LEARN

LIBRARY MANAGMENT

Dr. Anil Kumar Dhiman

and

Smt. Yashoda Rani

Ess Ess Publications

4837/24, Ansari Road, Darya Ganj,
New Delhi-110002
✆ : 23260807
Fax : 23274173
E-mail: info@essessreference.com
url:http://www.essessreference.com

First Published 2005

ISBN : 81-7000-448-9

Price : 300/-

Published by :

Ess Ess Publications

4837/24, Ansari Road, Darya Ganj,
New Delhi - 110 002
Phone : 23260807
Fax : 23274173
E-mail: info@essessreference.com
url:http://www.essessreference.com

Printed at :

Printline, New Delhi

Contents

Learning Library Science Series

Each book in this series has been written to provide in-depth knowledge of the basics of Library and Information Science and is in accordance with the B.Lib.Sc. syllabus of major Indian universities imparting the said course. To make this work series more comprehensible for the students, the books under this series have been written in Question-Answer format and the language used is very simple, easy and understandable. This series has been divided into six parts, each of which is dedicated to one basic aspect of library and information science.

The present series consists of six books in all, its first part deals with Learn Library and Society, second is Learn Library Management, third is Learn Library Classification (Theory), fourth being Learn Library Classification (Theory), fifth, Learn Reference Services, Information Services and Their Sources and the last and sixth book is Learn Computer Basics and its Application in Libraries. This gives a comprehensive and complete coverage to almost all the syllabi of most of the Indian universities imparting Bachelors' Degree in Library and Information Science (B.Lib.Sc.).

Although this book has primarily been written, keeping in mind the students making an attempt at the above mentioned Degree course, but it is hoped that this book shall find its place with anyone who is interested to know and learn more about the basics of library and information science. Not only the students, but the teachers of library and information science can derive equal benefit from this series. The books are equally suited to librarianship, library science students and library staff seeking to upgrade their skills.

Authors

Acknowledgements

It is indeed difficult to write one book and writing such a series of books is naturally much more difficult but this series could finally see the light of the day, but this could never have been possible without those innumerous books which have been consulted at every step and we are grateful to the authors of all those books, naming all of whom would not be humanly possible. We are thankful to Mrs. Sheel Sethi and Mr. Sumit Sethi, the owners of Ess Ess Publications for giving us an opportunity to present this voluminous work to the readers. We would also like to record our thanks to our friend, Mr. Sushil Kumar of IIT, Roorkee for his kind help. We feel indebted to Sh. Ram Lal Dhiman, Smt. Kamla Devi and Ms. Alka Rani who helped us at various steps. Last but not the least, we are thankful to our son Aman who could not get much of our attention while we were working on this work.

Anil. K. Dhiman
Yashoda Rani

1
Concept and Principles of Management and Administration

Q: Describe the principle of management, which should be kept in view in the assignment of duties to the staff in library.

Or

Explain the concept of "management" how it is different from administration and organization?

Or

Enunciate the general principles of management and their application to libraries.

Or

How are the general principles of management different from modern management?

Or

Justify the need and importance of the principles of scientific management in managing modern libraries.

Ans.: The term 'Management' has been variously defined by different authors. But one thing that most can agree upon is that the ultimate task of management is to guide people towards goal accomplishment.

C.W. Wilson has defined "Management is the process of realising and directing human agencies towards attaining a different goal."

John F.Meet defines management as "the art of securing maximum results with a minimum effort so as to secure maximum prosperity and happiness for both employee and give the public the best possible service."

According to *Henry Fayol* "To manage is to forecast and to plan, to organise, to command, to co-ordinate and to control."

Stanley Vance defines "Management simply as the process of decision-making and control over the action of human beings for the express purpose of attaining pre-determined goals".

Harold Koontz "Management is the art of getting things done through and with people in formally organized groups."

Henery L.Sisk quote "Management as the coordination of all the resources through the process of planning, organizing, directing and controlling in order to attain the stated objective".

From the above definitions, it is clear that the term management includes two basic concepts (i) it is concerned with achieving certain stated objectives; and (ii) it is the people who accomplish work. Accomplishment of the objectives through people becomes the role of an ideal manager. Management is now emerging as an independent discipline in the academic world.

Concept of Management

The nature of Management can be analysed in the context of its being an art or science.

There has been a controversy for many years over the concept of management. It is an art, which depends upon skill or it is a science, which depends upon analysis. According to *J.Paul Gatty*, "Management cannot be systematized or practised according to formula. It is an art, even a creative art". Others disagree, it is said that management is the oldest of arts and the youngest of sciences. This explains the changing nature of management.

Art is the know-how to accomplish a desired result. The art of management deals with the application of skill and effort to accomplish the stated objectives. Every art requires some principles, though they are no so rigid as scientific principles. Same is the case with management. A manager uses his skill and knowledge to solve the problems in an organization. Management gets perfection in the art of managing through continuous practice.

Science is a systematized body of knowledge which explain the cause and effect phenomenon with underlying principles which have unsual application. In this regard, management has developed certain principles laws and generalizations which are universal in nature and can be applied under similar circumstances of business environment.

Thus, management cannot be an exact science, because it deals with human beings. It may, however, be a combination of both art and science elements.

According to *Louis A Allen*, "Management" is a body of systematized knowledge based on general principles which are verifiable in terms of business which is the purview of administration.

As far as the organization is concerned it is the design of the structure, the grouping of positions, which will best-carry out the library's planned objectives. Orgnisation is the form of every human association for the attainment of common purpose. According to *Immelman* "Organization implies a structure of authority which requires a single directing executive authority and many workers". It involves the designing of the structure of authority, defining and classifying the post, their relationship with each other and ensuring proper correspondence for achieving the objectives of an organization.

Where as, administration involves the techniques by which the purpose of an orgnaisation is fulfilled at minimum cost with minimum efforts. Administration is, in fact, mainly concerned with the directive function through which an administrator unifies the efforts of all the individual engaged in an enterprise and guides their activities in the right direction.

According to *D.S Kimbell*, "Administration or direction is that function of management which actually executes or carries out the objectives for which the enterprise is organized".

Library Management

ALA Glossary of Library and Information Science defined library management as the process of coordinating total resources of an organization towards the accomplishment of desired goals of that organization through the execution of a group of inter-elated functions such as planning, organization, staffing, directing and controlling.

Further the *glossary* differentiates administration and management in the following way:

"So defined management is usually used synonymously with administration in current literature. Administration may be considered to be a broader term. Emphasizing the planning function, involving goal setting and major policy formulation, with management variously limited to the process of coordinating certain functions and activities of an organization toward the accomplishment of its goals."

Library Organization Vs. Library Administration

The distinction from each other can be stated as under:

1. Organization provides the structure of authority whereas administration actually uses devices for achieving the goal.
2. Organization is the machinery of the administration. Administration is concerned with the directive function.
3. An organization comes first and the administration follows it.
4. There can be no efficient administration unless there is a sound organization.
5. Administration starts the moment an organization is established. The administration of the library starts when the day-to-day working of the library is to be undertaken.

The difference between organization and administration is very subtle. In fact, both administration and organization are merely the machinery for attaining practice. The principles of management are flexible which can be used with modifications in different and changing situations.

Library Administration & Management

Library administration, as mentioned in *Harrods Librarians Glossory and Reference Book,* is the force behind the machinery of its working routine. To oversee the wok of a library in all its relations, and to plan for and promote its usefulness, is the work of the library administrator, and it embrasses the supervision and it embrasses the supervision and development of the work of all departments and the solution of their various problems; "library administration must of necessity being where library organization ends". Library management means the skill or manner of handling, controlling and directing the working of a library. In the words of *Girja Kumar* "there has been a qualitative change during the transition from library administration to library managements. The former is a narrower concept concerned with the set of rules to run the administration. It is atleast concerned with achieving results, improving the quality of human beings, raising the out put and generally improving the environment in which the system operates. The later is much broader concept viewing all operations strictly in term of results so hat a given input brings about maximum output and constantly results in improvements." The principles that govern library management are drawn much from management science as library administration was influenced in the beginning the principles of public administration.

Library management is not merely administering the routine works of the library, rather it is for achieving or accomplishing the objectives of the library. Therefore, a modern library requires more purposeful managerial concept rather than applying some traditional and outdated norms. Hence new kinds of tools, techniques and procedures has to be adopted for satisfactory performance of library service.

Principles of Management

The principles of management are the important factors which contribute to the success of any organization. It has a tremendous impact upon the practice of management in increasing the efficiency of the organization. The responsible administrator must know these principles and apply them with judgement in terms of his immediate situation. In view of its importance, scholars or management scientists have offered some view and propounded some fundamental principles. The principles of management are generalizations based on experience and careful analysis of case studies and are universally applicable.

Henri Fayol was the first to put forward a list of general administrative principles. On the whole, his observations are valid, even today. *Lyndally Urwick* examined the principles formulated by different authorities and succeeded in co-ordinating them into a unified system.

Henri Fayol is regarded as the father of classical school, sometimes, this schools is referred to as the "traditional" or "universalist" school. His principles are:

1. Division of work : In a small one-man library, one person would be carrying out all the functions such as ordering, classification, cataloguing, preparation, shelving, servicing of documents etc., there would be no division of work. But in a large library if all the professional assistants carry out all these functions, then this would lead to inefficiency and confusion. As the library grows, there should be a division of duties, and the activities. As division of work takes place it will lead to specialization. This is desirable in a large set up. Division of work should be carried out up to a point.

2. Authority : Authority can be either statutory or personal. Statutory authority belongs to a person due to his position. Personal authority is achieved due to qualities of leadership. Possession of authority means responsibility for actions. Actual work in the library may be done by different persons but the ultimate responsibilities lie with the chief librarian for all that goes on. He can delegate authority for a certain job. If the same is misused, then it can be withdrawn. An individual should be given authority equal to his responsibility. In case a person is given responsibility for a given job/task, then he should also be delegated authority to take necessary action to make it possible to fulfill the job/tasks successfully.

3. Discipline : In the best interest of the organization, there should be complete obedience, diligence, energy and outward marks of respect. This is equally applicable to every body. The best way to establish and maintain discipline is to provide good leadership to staff, dissolve disputes with justice and enforce penalties without prejudice.

4. Unity of command : An employee should be responsible to and also receive orders from only one superior. Any orders by the chief librarian to a professional assistant should be transmitted through an assistant librarian, who is incharge of the section. Thus, an organizational structure should be such that each employee is supervised by only one supervisor. He should be responsible for giving assignments to him and also assess his work. This principle protects an employee from awkward situations if he is supervised by two or more supervisors.

5. Unity of Direction : According to Fayol, there should be "one manager and one plan for all the operations which have the same objective in view". Unity of command depends on working of staff together properly but unity of direction is provided by means of properly arranging the organization so that there is one head and one plan to make it sure that coordinated effort would be achieved.

6. Subordination of Individual Interest to General Interest : According to this principle individual interests must be subordinated for the same of common good. Thus primary concern of an employee should be the growth and development of the organization. Head of the order section should not be permitted to take long leave during the last days of the financial year, if funds remain to be spent and bills have to be passed before the end of the financial year.

7. Remuneration : Salaries to employees and method of payment should be fair enough comparable to other staff of the parent body with equivalent qualifications. Employees should be given incentives for successful efforts.

8. Centralization : Centralization of administration may be carried out in varying degrees, depending upon the local situation. Anything that increases the importance of the role of a subordinate should be decentralized. On the other hand any thing that decreases the importance of the role of a subordinate should be centralized. In a university library, system of book selection should be highly decentralized because heads of departmental libraries know more about their fields of specialization than librarian of the central library. But ordering should be centralized so that there is no duplication of bibliographical tools, records and books. Managerial functions should be decentralized to a limited extent. As a result, the operation would improve and it would be possible to take advantage of the special knowledge acquired by the members of the staff working in departmental libraries.

9. Scalar Chain : This principle implies that authority and responsibility should flow in a clear unbroken line from the highest executive to the lowest rank. This refers to hierarchy, which consists of a series of steps, extending in a unbroken line from chief librarian to the lowest employee or an attendant. This line serves as a means of communication. Authority flows from superior to subordinates throughout the entire organization. Order go down along the line traveling from top to bottom. However information and appeal travel in the reverse direction.

10. Order : Order refers to the best possible arrangement to achieve the most efficient operation of the organization. As regards movement of materials, it would be economical if order section and cataloguing section are located side by side.

As regards employees, a right person must be given a right job most suitable to him. It would be a wrong decision to put an expert classifier in the maintenance section. A right place or job must be identified for everything and every individual.

11. Equity : In dealing with employees treatment of equality must be put into practice. Justice must be combined with friendliness and kindness by those in executive towards staff. Salary scales must be based on education, ability, experience and level of responsibility. Preferential treatment should be based on the question of superiority of a person in terms of the factors mentioned above.

12. Stability of Tenure : This principle is related to the staff's benefit. There should be stable and efficient work force for the survival of an organization. Frequent leaving of persons is expensive for the organization and reflects bad management. It must be corrected to ensure stability of efficient employees for longer duration in the organization.

In the library, it will better to fill up some positions in a library with medicore persons, who will stay with the library relatively for long period. At the same time there should be promotional avenues for competent persons also.

13. Initiative : It is concerned with thinking out and execution of a plan on the part of a manager or a worker. It minimises the period for completion of a particular project or a task. It promotes innovation, creativity and efficiency in the organization. As a positive gain, initiative must be encouraged at all levels in the organization.

14. Esprit De Corps : This principle refers to 'strength in unity' being an extension of principle of unity of command. Library administration should create environment which leads to harmony and unity. Equity, initiative, unity of command and leadership qualities of the senior staff can do much to promote esprit de corps. It requires team work. Communication is considered as the key to the satisfaction of a working group, resulting in team work .

Besides principles put forward by Fayol, other principles often included are span of control; coordination; line and staff; and accountability.

15. Span of Control : This refers to the number of persons with whom a manager must deal directly. There is no established criteria to determine how many individuals one manager can supervise efficiently. In practice the number of supervisors assigned to one manager vary usually from five to nine. However, in certain situations more than nine supervisors can be attached to one manager. This depends upon the kind of assignment allotted to different supervisors. In case nature of activities allocated to different units being supervised by a supervisor are similar in nature then the number of persons to be supervised by him can be increased. However, if the nature of activity varies then he would be able to supervise fewer persons efficiently.

16. Coordination : Coordination is very important in running an organization. It may be regarded as the essence of managership. If work of periodical section and documentation section is not coordinated, then this will lead to problems. Aim of coordination being to achieve harmony of individual efforts towards accomplishment of group goals. The manager reconciles differences of interest, efforts etc. to accomplish goals.

17. Line and Staff : Persons belonging to line positions are decision makers. They should possess authority and command. Staff positions are those which do not carry authority. These are advisory positions meant for providing information, advise and counsel. Such persons are not delegated authority and decision makers are not obliged to accept the advise given by them. A chief librarian can ask head of a section for information and advise because of his special knowledge but the chief may accept his advise or not. Now a days a staff unit may be a system analyst, a research unit, a public relations office, etc.

18. Accountability : In case, a library has to be run efficiently, then emphasis should be on measurement of quality and quantity of performance. The measurement of performance can be used towards accountability of an employee.

The principles of management are universally applicable. These are flexible and not absolute. These are applicable regardless of changing conditions and these form basis of scientific management.

Modern Management

Modern Management emphasises the complete employee view by revisionist researcher which includes systems theory, contingency theory, organizational humanism and management science. It is characterized by a scientific approach, which involves:

* The application of scientific methods and analysis to managerial functions and problems;
* Serious consideration of human elements in management, based on psychological studies and behaviour analysis in different situations;

* Increasing emphasis on economic effectiveness in all management functions;
* A systems approach, focusing equal attention on all functions of management; and
* Use of electronic computers for analysis and studies.

The principle of management listed above have been recognized by librarians. The application of scientific management based on these is in beginning to be used in libraries. Librarians seem to be showing more interest in this area of study and application. However, it is true that librarians have been slow to accept these ideas.

Q.: Define management and discuss its different schools of thought.

Ans. Management is an activity that converts disorganized human and physical resources into useful and effective results. It is a distinct process consisting of activities of planning, organising, actuating and controlling, performed to determine and accomplish stated objectives with the use of human beings and other resources. There are six basic resources: men, materials, machines, methods, money and market. These resources are utilized by four fundamental functions, viz., planning, organising, actuating and controlling to achieve the objectives.

Management exist in every of human organization. We all are affected by good or bad management practices, and we should therefore lean to recognise and influence the quality of management that affects our lives. The management makes human efforts more productive. It brings better equipments, plants, offices, products, services and human relations to our society. It brings order to endeavors by combing isolated events and disjoint information into meaningful relationships. These relationship then work to solve problems and accomplish goals.

During the past centuries, certain schools of management thoughts have been evolved. Each school centres the management concept around various elements involved. For example, the classical school centres round the concept of 'universalist' or 'traditional nature'; the scientific management school links rewards and motivation for work; the social system school deals with 'contribution-satisfaction equilibrium'; the psycho-sociological school tries to relate 'individuals to their abilities' and the human emotions and other factors that underlie the process of organization. Human behaviour and motivation school is of the view that working conditions have a great role to play in production; and management styles group is of the opinion that a complex of issues like leadership, motivation, decision-making, right and timely communication play an important role in management process.

Major schools of management theory may be classified as follows :-

1. **Scientific Schools** : Scientific schools include scientific management school and classical school.
2. **Human relation schools:** Human relations schools include human behaviour school and social system schools.
3. **Decision Theory Schools.**

1. Scientific Schools

These are further sub-divided into scientific management school and classical school.

(a) Scientific Management School : This schools uses the scientific method to obtain desired objectives in the workplace. The scientific method uses the following steps to achieve an objective:

1. Identify the objective;
2. Acquire information about the objective through observation;
3. Formulate an hypothesis about the objective;
4. Investigate the objective thoroughly by controlled experiments;
5. Set priority and clarify the data obtained;
6. State the tentative solution to the objective; and
7. Adjust and implement the answer to the objective.

Frederick W. Taylor has been called the father of scientific management. He believed that management, not labour, was the cause of and potential solution to problems in an organization. Taylor called for a mental revolution to fuse the interests of labour and management into a mutually rewarding whole. This mental revolution was based on four vital principles:

1. the development of the best work method,
2. the scientific selection and development of workers,

3. the relation and bringing together of the best work method and the developed and trained worker, and
4. the close cooperation of managers and non-managers, which include the division of work and manager's responsibility for planning the work.

Taylor had many disciples that spread the gospel of efficiency. Carl Barth, Henry Gantt, Frank Gilberth, Harrington Emerson, and Morris Cooke all made valuable written and practicing contributions to the growth of management as a scientific discipline.

(b) Classical School : This school was developed in France. This school is referred to as the "traditional" or "universalist" school. It regards management as a universal process. The management process is analyzed, conceptual framework is established, principles are identified and theory of management is built from it. Henry Fayol, a Frenchman is considered as the father of the classical school. He applied scientific approach but looked at administration from the top to down.

The principles of administration of Fayol are:

1. **Division of Work** : Fayol has advocated division of work to take the advantage of specialization. As division of work takes place, it leads to development of specialization.
2. **Authority and Responsibility** : Responsibility is corollary of authority. He finds authority as continuation of official and personal factors. In order to discharge the responsibility properly, there should be parity of authority and responsibility.
3. **Discipline** : The personnel serving in an organization should be disciplined.. Discipline may be of two types *self imposed discipline* and *command discipline.*
4. **Unity of command** : Under this principle, the sub-ordinate should receive order from one senior only. It is considered as an important aspect in managing an organization.
5. **Unity of Direction** : According to this principle, each group of activities with the same objective must have one head and one plan. Unity of direction provides better coordination among various activities to be undertaken by an organization.
6. **Subordination of Individual to General Interest** : This principle advised that common interest is above the individual interest. Individual interest must be subordinated to general

interest when there is conflict between the two. Any kind of self interest must be reduced.

7. **Remuneration of Personnel** : Remuneration of employees should be fair and provided maximum possible satisfaction to employees and the employers.
8. **Centralization** : Everything which goes to increase, the importance of subordinate's role is decentralized, every thing which goes to reduce, it is centralized. So, there should be centralization of authority.
9. **Scalar chain** : There should be scalar chain of authority and of communication ranging from the highest to the lowest. It suggests that each communication going up or coming down must flow through each position in the line of authority and should be unbroken line of authority. For this purpose, Fayol has suggested '*gang plank*' which is used to prevent the scalar chain from bogging down action.
10. **Order** : According to this principle there should be a place for every thing and every thing should be in its place.
11. **Equity** : Equity is the combination of justice and kindness. In dealing with subordinate equity is essential.
12. **Intiative** : Within the limits of authority and discipline, managers should encourage their employees for taking initiatives. Initiative is concerned with thinking out and execution of a plan.
13. **Stability of Tenure** : No employee should be removed within short time. Unnecessary turnover is both cause and effect of bad management.
14. **Esprit de corps** : This principle emphasizes team work and the importance of effective communication in achieving the same.

2. Human Relations Schools

The human relation schools consider that as managing involves getting things done through people, therefore management studies should be evolved around interpersonal relations. Thus the main emphasis is on the individual and the informal group in the formal organization. The basic concern is to study people as human beings rather than as mere work units. Sociologists and psychologist have been very active in developing these schools of thought.

(a) Human Behaviour School : The focus of the Human Behaviour School is on behaviour of the individual, the group, and the organization. This theory looks at the human factor as the central theme. It lays greater emphasis on interpersonal relations, leadership, group dynamics and motivation of personnel. The basic assumption is that in case the management can keep the employees happy, then this will result in the maximum performance.

Follett emphasized the psychological and sociological aspects of management. She looked a management as a social process and felt that coordination was the most important principle.

In 1930s, *Elton Mayo* and group of industrial psychologists conducted experiments at the Western Electric Hawthrone Plant in Chicago. They came to the conclusion that social interaction and psychologcal factors are important in determining the level of productivity and satisfaction.

(b) Social System School : The Social System School encourages employees to develop social groups on the job, to participate in management and allows democratic functioning in the enterprise. *Chester Barnard* has written about contribution-satisfaction equilibrium. He has identified four specific inducements. He regards communication as the first function of a manager.

In 1950s, *Peter Drucker* introduced "Management by Objectives". He has been supported by *Douglas Mc Gregor* in his "Theory Y". *Abraham Maslow* has further built up his "Need Theory". According to it, man has a hierarchy of needs starting with lowest needs (physiological needs-food, shelter, and clothing), ultimately proceeding to highest needs (intangible needs-self-actualizing and fulfillment). He concluded that when one set of needs was satisfied, then that kind of needs ceased to be a motivator. His identification of basic needs has been fairly popular but hierarchical aspects of his theory has been questioned.

3. Decision Theory School

These schools perceive management in terms of decision-making. These are primarily concerned with the study of rational decision procedures and also the way managers actually reach decision. Major contribution in this approach has come from Simon. Other contributors are March, Cyert, Forrester, etc. The major emphasis of this approach is that decision making is a decision-making unit. Therefore, the basic problem in managing is to make rational decision. From this point of view, decision theory approach has the following features:-

1. Management is essentially decision making.
2. The members of the organization are decision-makers and problem-solvers.
3. Quality of decision affects the organizational effectiveness.
4. All factors affecting decision-making are the subject-matter of study of management.

In Decision - theory, the inbuilt assumption being that mathematical models and quantitative processes can serve as a basis of all management.

So it is seen that different schools of management thought have provided different versions regarding management creating confusion. Classical school regards management as a universal process. The behaviourists consider human factor as the central theme, which simply involves interpersonal relations. Some consider management simply as decision making. However, the different schools of management thought are interrelated and are concerned with management process.

Q. : Describe in detail the elements of management and their applications in the effective management of a library.

Ans: Every organization or institution has a set of goals to achieve. For this an organizational structure is raised, an administrative machinery is created and management authority is appointed. The basic policies of the organization are laid down and management staff is appointed by the administrative machinery for achieving the desired goals.

To ensure better functioning and smooth running of an organization, *Luther Gulick* propounded some basic elements of management on the pattern of Fayol principles of management. These are known as 'POSDCORB' which stands for the following seven elements:-

1. Planning
2. Organising
3. Staffing

4. Directing
5. Co-ordinating
6. Reporting
7. Budgeting

1. Planning: The primary function of an administrator is to plan and forecast, i.e., determining the goal and ideas of an institution. Planing presupposes the stock-taking of the existing conditions and the relevant causes. The solutions are suggested for removing the problems by a phased programme. The efforts are made to remove the basic defects and their future implications are taken care of. Same is the case with Library Planing.

2. Organising: Planing to be fruitful needs a sound organization, which means such a structure of authority is established which is capable of achieving the set goals. Through this structure, work-subdivisions are arranged, defined and coordinated for the set goal. In Library Organization, the decision is taken as to what kind of authority is to be provided for an area of service.

3. Staffing: An organization for its efficiency needs proper staffing and recruitment policies. Practical experience of various jobs at the credit of applicants for various posts should be taken in to consideration at the time of appointment. Staffing includes the training of staff and maintenance of favourable conditions of work for them. The Chief Librarian should be a qualified and competent person with an aptitude of research.

4. Directing: The efficiency of the staff depends upon the personal qualities of the Chief Librarian. He should be capable of performing his duties as a leader. Besides, possessing knowledge, he should be able to infuse confidence amongst the staff-members. He should prove an ideal leader by din of his hard work, sincerity for the welfare of the staff. Directing includes continuous decision making and translate theme in orders and instructions.

5. Co-ordinating : It is essential to inter-relate various parts of an organization in a harmonious way. The co-ordination can be achieved if the head knows about all the jobs and effects such an administrative machinery that he feels practically no necessity to interfere. It depends upon the kind of organization which has been brought in to being, as to wheather there is line type or line and staff type of structure or functional type of organization. There should be delegation of powers or proper functioning, but they should be answerable to the chief only.

6. Reporting : It means keeping the library authorities well informed about the progress or regress of the work. The chief of the library has to submit an annual report to executive authority concerned. This practice keeps the Chief Librarian vigilant about his activities. Various section Heads of the Library may maintain proper records and statistics of the work performed for the purpose.

7. Budgeting : It includes fiscal planning, accounting and control. No organization can function properly without adequate finances. Librarian has to convince the authorities about the usefulness of the services rendered by libraries.

This can be done by statistical data only so the Librarian should maintains proper statistics of income and expenditure of his Library. He should ensure proper utilization of financial grants. Budgeting should be made in a presentable form with solid justification.

Mr. Mohinder Singh has added a few more elements.

1. Creating (before planning)
2. Motivating (after staffing)
3. Communicating (before directing)
4. Controlling (after coordinating).

Briefly, these are discussed below –

1. Creating : Creativeness is one of the vital functions of management. A creative manager can make an organization itself creative. Through his creative approaches of logical thinking, idea-linking and problem solving, he can create new and better ways of achieving objectives. Creative function adds innovation and improvement in the activities and procedures of the organization.

2. Motivating : Motivating is a valuable function of management. Motivated people only achieve set goals. In an organization, people at all levels should be motivated by way of giving proper stimuli to them so as to achieve desired behaviour. Only desired behaviour leads towards accomplishment of organizational objectives. Individuals are motivated by satisfying their five-tiers of needs as recognised by A H Maslow-Physiological Needs relating to maintenance of life (e.g. food, air, water, rest, etc.) and economic security relating to job protection, salary deduction, fine, etc.; Social Needs relating to form associations, friendships, etc.; Esteem Needs relating to enjoyment of status, recognition, appreciation, self-respect and freedom; and Self-realisation Needs relating to self-fulfilment or continued self-development.

3. Communicating : Communicating is also an important element of the management chain. Communication creates co-ordination and participation in the management. Through communication, managers transfer the message, may it be facts, ideas, attitudes or opinions in all directions, to all concerned executives and subordinates to influence a particular course of action to achieve a pre-planned common goal or objective. The communication may be formal or informal. It may flow in any direction upwards, as suggestion from subordinate to superior, downwards as orders or instructions from superior to subordinate and laterally as an information flow for necessary action or correction among concerned executive across the lines of an organization.

4. Controlling : Controlling is the process by which management gauges the progress of work against set targets. In other words, controlling compares events with plans and makes necessary corrections where events have deviated from plans. In management, budget provides inherent control over plans. In a business type management, break-even analysis, where profits or losses are measured at different volume levels of sales, is another controlling technique. This concept in the form of cost-benefit analysis can also be profitably applied to a service-type organization, like a library or information centre. Leadership of a manager also plays an important role in controlling employee in behaviour in an organization. He feeds checking, regulation, verification and overall supervision to actions for achieving desired objectives.

Q. : Write short notes on :

1. Participative Management

2. Performance Appraisal

3. Total Quality Management (TQM)

Ans.

1. Partcipative Management

Decision making is an important management process in any organization. Without decision, nothing can be properly planned or accomplished. Decisions may be simple and with sufficient foresight - or complex and with lack of foresight. Modern management techniques encourage the use of participative decision making, stressing that productive and efficient results can come out of this decision making process.

The management technique which allows its employees, individuals or groups to take part in decision making is known as participative management.

Since participative management pushes decision making down to lower levels, the higher level officials need to develop their competence, expertise and experience. It does not believe in punishment as a tool of control. The group is supportive of the individuals/employees comprising it and intended to fulfil the organizational objectives. In the process of decision making, the participation of staff is considered from various aspects such as:

(a) What are the systems of participation at present?

(b) Are people involved in issues that affect them?

(c) Are they being consulted specifically when a vital decision is being taken (e.g., Application of Information Technology)?

(d) Is involvement early enough or regular enough?

The involement of staff in the decision making process of the organization and having increased awareness of the organization's purpose, depend upon two important factors: (i) Leadership (ii) Organizational Style.

(i) Leadership : Leadership behaviours lead to highly motivated staff. Subordinates rely upon the leadership skills of their superiors to show them how to achieve their needs of motivation, rewards and ability to perform their allocation tasks. Leaders resolve interpersonal differences. Formal systems are simplified and attempts are made to create a more open, reactive organizational environment. The need for leadership qualities turns more towards the ability to get people to interact. The capacity to mediate is very important, and the ability to plan and analyse feedback is emphasized. The leader's role is not diminished but it is changed in its nature. Participative leadership involves employee participation in management. Subordinates are consulted for their opinions as part of the decision-making process.

(ii) Organizational Style : Whether the participative approach can really work depends upon the type of organization and its functioning. An open organization is more likely to encourage participative management than a mechanistic one. The emphasis in organizational communication from top to bottom through informal, group, team and party meetings is laid on self-starting qualities, the capacity of staff to develop themselves in their own jobs and to grow professionally. The organizational style of functioning should encourage that people at work need to satisfy their higher level needs, for success, self respect and self-actualization, as well as their basic needs for material support and security. Participative decision making has its effect on the organization's objectives.

Advantages and Disadvantages of Participative Management

Advantages : For improving the library and information service, the management follows the technique of participatory decision making which has got the following advantages.

(1) **High Productivity :** Participative Management assures high productivity in the sense that involvement of staff in the decision making process provides one and all good working condition, motivation, and ability to work and introduce the desired result in time. The outcome of the decisions is always target oriented to meet the goals and objectives of the organization. It taps the talents, the ideas, the knowledge and the skills of individuals who might not otherwise be included in the decision making process.

(2) **Superior Quality:** Participative Management stresses that higher quality decisions and quality of library services often result from these practices. Decisions are found to be superior especially if the group is composed of individuals of different areas of expertise with a common need for solution.

(3) **Wider Acceptability :**Group decisions tend to be more readily accepted by the group. Participative decision making is also useful for resolving differences among group members. The decisions are acceptable to all groups or individuals.

Disadvantages : There are also disadvantages to participative decision-making.

(1) Implementation of the tough decisions taken by the management

through participative decision-making sometimes stalls the entire activities taking the problem form one committee to another committee.

(2) Group decision-making can be expensive in terms of staff time. A group decision normally takes more time than an executive action. In order to estimate the full cost of partcipative decision-making the decision-making time should be multiplied by the number of people attending the group meeting.

(3) Lower quality decisions are also expected through participative decision-making which is not truly effective. If superiors are present or if one member has a dominant personality, the decision of the group may in reality not be a group decision. This can have a lowering effect on group morale and of a negative factor for motivation making for feelings of frustration and uselessness.

2. Performance Appraisal (PA)

When we look back at the history of management, we find that management has undergone several changes and it can be divided into Pre-scientific Era, Scientific Era and Human Relation Era. Human relation is the process of effective motivation of individuals in a given situation so as to achieve greater human satisfaction and accomplishment of desired goals. There are various techniques of management which can be applied to any organization, such as Bureaucratic Management, Participative Management, Management by Objectives and Total Quality Management etc.

Performance appraisal is the process by which an employee's contribution to an organization during a specific time period is assessed. And it can be effectively used to improve employee motivation and performance, if used properly and can lead to disastrous conditions if used inapproperiately. It is a multi-component process of identifying, observing, measuring and developing human performance in organization. Where, the identification is the process of determining what areas are to be focused on which job analysis is required as a means of identifying performance scale. The observation indicates that all appraisal criteria must be sufficiently observed so that a fair and accurate judgement can be made. Observations on infrequent and non-performance characteristics may lead to poor ratings. The measurement is the central feature of appraisal. The evaluater must some how translate the observations into value judgement representing the level of subjects. The development suggests that performance appraisal should also focus on improving future performance.

Objective of PA

The following are the objectives of good performance appraisal systems:

* Facilitating integrated growth of employee.
* Helping employees to know their strengths and weaknesses and thus enable them to improve performance of self and organization.
* Helping the creation of an enabling organization where opportunities are available for fuller utilisation of the known potentials of the employees. The climate of such an organization is one of the mutuality, trust, collaboration and openness, etc.
* Generating valid data about employees for personnel functions like training, placement, selection and promotion etc.
* Providing feedback and guidance by the superior to the employees for improvement of their performance.

Purposes of PA

The following may be the purposes of performance appraisal :

* Administrative decisions, such as promotion, transfers and allocation of financial rewards etc.
* Employee's development, i.e., identification of training needs and performance feedback etc.
* Personnel research, such as generation of manpower information for salary and wages determination, career planning, man-job matching promotion, helping supervisors to know their subordinates and also to help subordinates to assess their achievement and failure etc.

Characteristic Needs of a Good Performance Appraisal System

A good performance appraisal system would have the following characteristics:

* The organization believes that development of employees is in its own interest.

* The organization will provide opportunities and conditions for the development and optimization of human resources.
* The corporate management is willing to invest adequate time and resources for the development of employees.
* Managers have concern for the growth of subordinates.
* Employees are willing to avail the given opportunities for growth and receive necessary help from the managers for their development and improving performance.

Types of Performance Appraisal

Following two types of the performance appraisal system are determined. These are :

(i) Cost Centred Appraisal System and (ii) Objective Centred Appraisal System.

Of these, the first one is meant for profit making organizations and second one is meant for non-profit making organizations. Since, library and information centres are primarily non-profit making organizations, hence the objective centred appraisal can be implemented in these centres.

Performance appraisal System in LIS Centres

As stated earlier, this is the most neglected and under-used technique of management in the library and Information fields. But the following points ensure why performance appraisal is needed in library and information centres:

1. To ascertain the definition of the work or job to be performed as there is an urgent need for clear demarcation of the jobs.
2. Wherever amenable, we should establish acceptable performance standard in terms of specific measurable desired behaviour. This calls for defining units of job, the time taken for doing the job and the modes of performing these jobs.
3. To identify the present performance level of the library staff in terms of specific measurable behaviour which is considered to be desirable or acceptable.
4. To identify the needed improvement in library staff behaviour consistent with the objective of library services.
5. To provide a basis of feedback for the performance of library staff in differences.

3. Total Quality Management (T Q M)

T Q M is concerned with the integration of all efforts in the organization towards quality and customer care.

- One objective: continuous improvement;
- Three principles: customer focus, process improvement and total involvement and
- Six supporting elements: leadership, education and training, a supportive structure, communications, reward and recognition and measurement.

TQM is defined as the management approach of an organization centered on quality, based on participation of all its members and aiming at a long term success through customer satisfaction and benefits to all members of the organization and to society.

Principles of TQM

The management scientists have derived certain principles from the philosophy to TQM concept and they can be described as follows:

1. Leadership : Effective leadership is the foundation for TQM. Top management should provide the leadership for quality awakening in the organization. They should evolve effective plans and provide leadership in achieving the objectives.

2. Internal and External Customers : The external customers are the outsiders who buy the organization's products or services. The internal customers are the staff of the organization including those not in direct contact with the external customers. These staff interact with other staff as they are involved in dispensation of services of the organization. In this way the customer organization can pervade the organization.

3. Customer Satisfaction : The customer has to decide what the standards should be and not the supplier/producer. If the organization decides the standards, the product may not satisfy the customer's requirements. Therefore, quality is customer defined.

4. Performance Measurement : Performance measurement needs to be based upon timely measures and feedback on performance through superior quality information systems.

5. Measure of Success : Every organization has to define what is the criterion for success in their operations and how to measure it.

For instance, one of the measures is sales of products and the resulting profits. Thought is difficult to measure the customer's satisfaction, it can be measured through indirect indicators such as increased sales, repeated orders, exports, etc.

6. Continuous Improvement : Continuous improvement should be the responsibility of everyone in the organization. The organization should not be satisfied with one time success. It should aim at sustaining success through continuous improvement, because customers will expect still better services and products.

7. Essential Training and Education : The Manual specifies the jobs and what they are supposed to do and how they can do them. The employee should be educated and trained in their trade otherwise they cannot understand the documentation and manuals.

8. Communication : Right communication is to be maintained to carry out the jobs in the right way. Manuals and other such documentations help to achieve proper communication. The organization should also improve communications through newsletters, notice-boards, problem solving sessions and departmental meetings etc.

9. Attitudes towards Quality : Every employee should develop an attitude to improve the quality of the organization.

10. Team Work : The organization has to make every effort to mould the employees to work as a team. It is the only way through which an organization can achieve its objective and practice of TQM. Recognition of achievements is also equally essential for the success of TQM programme.

11. Employee Involvement : Employee involvement means that each individual must take the initiative and rely upon someone else. To achieve this, the organization needs a culture which encourages this behaviour. Everyone must understand that they contribute equally and can only succeed through co-operation and support.

Benefits of TQM

In the light of the aforesaid elaboration of the concept of TQM, the following benefits can be derived:

(i) Work itself becomes more interesting through a greater involvement of employees.

(ii) Increase in general productivity.

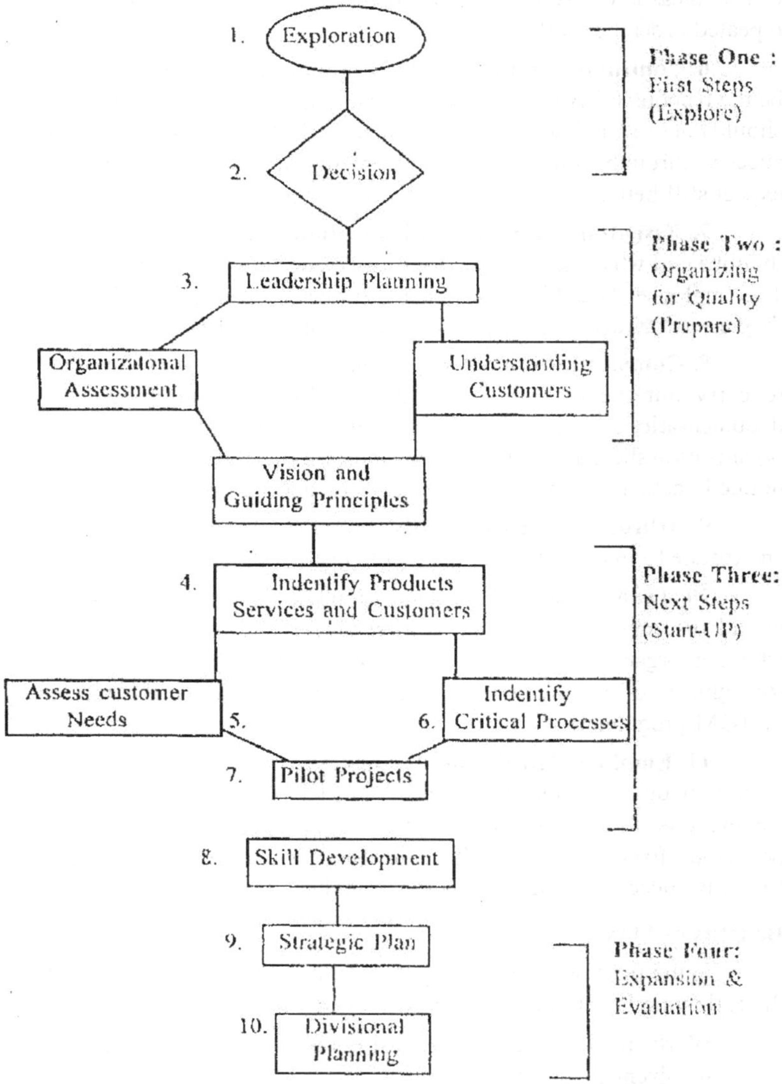

Fig. Total Quality Management : Library Implementation Model

(iii) Less absenteeism because of greater interest in job satisfaction to employees.

(iv) Fewer grievances among the employees; and

(v) All-round greater team spirit

Thus, all these aspects of TQM are to be understood by every employee so that they can create a new culture that leads to a great success of the organization.

TQM in Library and Information Centres

Allthough. TQM is a new concept in management but it is equally beneficial to each and every organization including service organization like library. Dr S.R. Ranganathan's fourth law a library science, 'Save the time of the readers' has similar implications to what is advocated in TQM approach. Since the beginning of 1990s, some of Library and Information Centres had started to think about TQM after a growing awarencess of the relevance of quality management methods to provide pinpointed, exhaustive, expenditious and efficient information to the users but still it is not being taken into consideration very seriously. TQM can be seen on two groups of libraries viz., (i) those whose parental organization are adopting TQM and (ii) the library and information services.

The users are the ultimate judge of the quality of the services being provided by a library & information centre. User satisfaction and continuos improvement of the services are the two primary goals of a library. By applying TQM technique, the librarians can not only satisfy the users consistently as per their needs and requirements but also improve quality of their services regularly. TQM in a Library & Information Centre may helps in:

* better product design;
* developing an inventory of all the documents available in a library;
* developing a database which includes records for all types of material held in library;
* facilitating through a variety of tools that can provide access to universal publications;
* improving quality of information analysis and consolidation product;

* improving skills of end users to profitability interact with information system and services;
* integrating and networking all library resources into serviceable resources to users;
* reduction of user complaints;
* efficient utilization of men, machines and materials, resulting in higher productivity;
* elimination of bottlenecks and tension free work environment leading to good human relations; and
* improvement of confidence among users.

2
Collection Development

Q. : Write on essay on collection development in libraries.

Ans. The basic components of the library are books, people and building and the heart of the library lies in its collection. Collection development is the first and foremost function of any library. The term "Collection Development" includes all such activities as assessing the user needs, evaluating the present collection, determining the selection policy, co-ordinating, the selection of items, re-evaluating and storing parts of the collection, and planning for resource sharing. Thus collection development is not a single activity but a group of activities. Acquisition is usually distinguished from collection development. Acquisition refers to the process of verifying ordering and making the payment for the required materials.

Joseph C. Shipman has defined collection development as "the sum total of library materials; books, manuscripts, serials, government documents, pamphlets and microfiche, punched cards, computer tapes etc. that make up the holdings of a particular library. In other words, it is planned, systematic development of an already existing collection".

According to *Mosher*, collection development is "the effective and timely selection of library materials forming carefully constructed area or subject collection, shaped over time by bibliographic experts. It is the synopsis linking thousands of decisions to sensitive provision of needed research materials, the capacity to make the parts fit the needed whole."

Collection development is sometimes considered as synonymous to "collection Building" which means that there is already nucleus of collection in the library and the librarian is going to build up the collection. But collection development is a term other than collection building. Since the word development implies qualitative improvement of the collection. That is why Shipman has said "Building a collection may occasionally involve the selection and acquisition of... materials *ab initio* but in most cases it is likely to mean the planned systematic development of an already existing collection."

Therefore, the collections have to be built systematically and continuously. It is said that developing the collection is one of the most important and responsible activities in the library. In fact, the utilisation of library depends upon the quality of its collection. So, librarian has to be play a significant role in developing collection. The collection development in libraries has to be done on sound principles, only then the library can succeed in meeting its defined aims.

Objectives of Collection Development

The objective of collection development is to build a library collection which will supply a continuously expanding store of useful information to support and enrich the programs of its parent organization. In order to provide the best materials for the implementation of its duties, the library requires guidelines for collection development. The policies which are, of necessity, subject to review as needed, form the framework for building the library's collection.

Collection development is a plan which can be implemented and evaluated. It is a process of intertwining of (i) information resources (ii) information use and user demands and (iii) fiscal resources. The process involves mainly three aspects.

(i) Collection planning;

(ii) Collection implementation; &

(iii) Collection evaluation.

Figure shown on next page illustrates the interrelationship between information resources, information use and library on one hand and the process of collection development, its dependance on collection planning, collection implementation and collection evaluation on the other. While collection planning is a design for acquiring documents as determined by the needs, goals and objectives of the library. Collection implementation is the process of making documents accessible for use and collection evaluation connotes examining and judging the relevance in relation to goals and objectives.

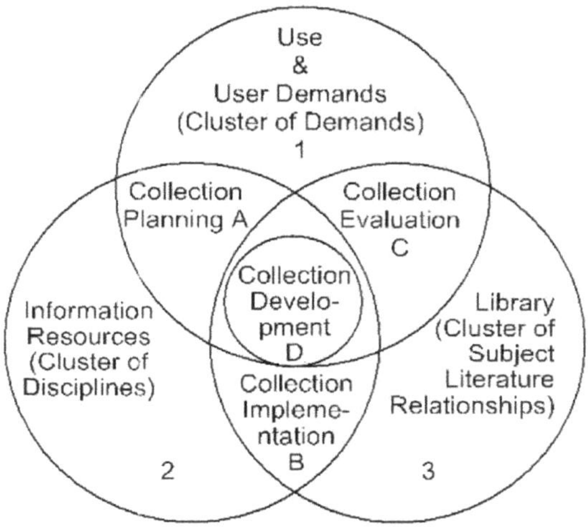

Collection Development : A Structural Approach

Collection Development Policy

It is the course of action adopted for developing the collection or stock in a library. A policy can be unwritten convention or a written document. The American Library Association's Collection Development Committee when preparing "*Guidelines for the formation of collection development policies*" assumed that 'a written collection development policy is for any library a desirable tool which enables selectors to work with grater consistency towards defined goals, thus shaping stronger collections and using limited funds more wisely."

A written collection developments policy is preferred to non-written policy. A Collection Development Policy consists of following:

A. Responsibility for Selection

In the academic environment, selection of library materials is a joint responsibility of teaching faculty and the library professional staff. The primary responsibility for the co-ordination of the collection development process lies with the Collection Development Librarian. While recommendations from teaching faculty are welcomed and solicited, the library professional staff will carry the responsibility for ordering in areas not covered by faculty (e.g. Reference, General, etc.) and/or the remaining budget not yet encumbered, so as to achieve a balanced collection, and to make sure that the total allocated budget is encumbered. The ultimate responsibility for collection development direction and policy decisions, including adequacy and quality of selections, rests with the Library Director, and, under his or her direction, with the Collection Development Librarian.

B. Factors to Consider in Selection

In selecting materials for the library, factors to be considered are as follows:

1. The permanent or timely value of the material for interest, information, or enlightenment.
2. The accuracy of the material.
3. The usefulness of the material with respect to other materials already in the collection.
4. The probable usage of the material in the educational and research mission of the University/Institute.
5. For serials, priority for titles that are analysed in standard indexing and/ or abstracting services to which the library provides access, for support of subject areas with new degree programs, for deficiencies indicated by comparison studies with other universities, and/or for access to a title unavailable in the document delivery system when the requested title is to support a new degree program.

C. Materials to be Acquired

The library will acquire, as far as funds permit, all materials needed to support the teaching and research programs of the University/ Institute. Due to the diversity, extent, and unique character of research endeavours, it is not financially feasible to build a collection comprehensive enough to support all research interests. Electronic database searching, networking, and Interlibrary Loans (ILL) are among the alternative methods, which may be considered in providing access to research materials. A limited number of current publications of popular appeal and interest may be selected from an approved list of Best Seller books. The majority of materials acquired will include monographs, sets, maps, journals and other serial publications, newspapers, pamphlets, photo reproductions, government documents, microforms, archival materials, manuscripts, audiovisual materials, and other items commonly included as part of library resources, except for special textbooks and juvenile collections, the library will not normally purchase materials to be used solely for classroom instruction such as cliff notes, study guides, etc.

D. Budgetary Considerations

Budget allocations are not made specifically to departments independent of the library. The procedures followed in allocating funds to the various subject areas may be based on a formula with various factors, such as number of students enrolled at various levels, number of courses. Offered in each discipline during a particular semester, circulation records, and average price of book in each discipline considered. A copy of the formula for monograph allocations is available at the Collection Development Office. Exceptions are made for subject areas where there are extra funds available through special line item accounts.

E. Format

All books will be ordered in whatever format is requested by Librarians/ Faculty members. In case the format is not identified, books will be ordered in hard copy. If the requested format is not available, whatever available format will be ordered in hard copy, unless it is specified otherwise by the Reference Librarian.

Advantages of CD

A Collection Development Policy :

1. Expresses openly its relationship with the objectives of the parent organization.
2. Forms the basis for planning collection development.
3. Provides practical guidance in day to day selection of reading materials free from personal bias.
4. Helps in determining the best method of acquisition.
5. Supports and assists in justifying the selection / collection. Collection Development policy offers some help against censorship by a clear statement of the type of materials to be purchased and indicating that the policy has the support of the library authority/committee.
6. Acts as a rational guide for budget allocation and also helps in long range budget planning by stating priorities and outlining growth and development goals.

7. Helps in making best use of resources.
8. Facilitates cooperative programmes like inter-library loans, resource sharing and network.
9. Assists in establishing methods of reviewing materials before purchase.
10. Offers suggestions on types of materials to be sorted, weeded and discarded.

Evaluation of Collection

Evaluation of the library collection is one of the major functions of collection development programme. In traditional methods, the following measures are usually considered for evaluating collection :

* Size of the collection : absolute size, size of the rare collection, size of subject, date, language, etc.,
* Number of volumes per user, number of volumes per document circulated, current growth rate, etc.,
* Amount of collection used; and
* Expenditure on collection, etc.

All these measures are inadequate to evaluate a library in the context of recent advances in IT. In addition to the above, the following measures are equally important in the modern context:

* Availability of CD-ROM databases : number of CD-ROM databases subject-wise, frequencey of updation, availability of CD-ROM drives, possibility of its remote access, availability of multimedia databases, etc.
* Access to internet success rate : how much is really accessed, number of records accessed and downloaded, number of accesses to other electronic publications, response time, the cost of accessing, Internet and other electronic publications through on-line services, etc.

It is difficult to collect such data since users can directly access such information through their terminals; librarians may not come to know such events. Eventually each of the users may have his/her own 'digital library' at very high cost and the library may become virtually non-existent.

One aspect of evaluating collection is keeping track of what is missing and what should be replaced. Replacement decisions may be based on reports of requested items not located and on visual inspection of documents that have been returned. Further, a sample of the collection can be surveyed to establish which subjects are sustaining the greatest losses. The other aspect of evaluation is to identify less used document so that they can be sent to a less expensive building for storing, or can be put into compact storage in a less accessible area of the main library building.

But in the context of IT, it is not that easy to measure the use of electronic records although, it may comparatively be easy to collect the data. It requires entirely a different mission to keep track of frequently used records and organise infrequently used records effectively in distributed text-based systems.

Weeding Policy

Weeding documents means removing documents which are found not usefjul or not serviceable from a library. The documents so removed from the library a may be completely discarded where they are not serviceable; are donated to some other library where they may be useful; or kept in a reserve place called a dormitory library. Weeding policy means a policy statement on (a) what materials are to be weeded; (b) when to weed; (c) who should weed; (d) how to weed; (e) what to do with weeded materials ?

(a) Purpose

The purpose of deselecting (weeding) is to assimilate a useful collection. Materials, which are no longer relevant to the funding of the library as well as materials which are in poor condition, are candidates for deselection.

(b) General Criteria

Unnecessary items left in a collection can weaken a library, as do insufficient acquisitions. Qutdated and shabby materials should obvisously be removed. Material not actively used in the library may also be considered for withdrawal from the collection, as these items may no longer be of use to library users. Specific Criteria for Consideration for Removal are :

1. duplicate copies that have had not more than one circulation in the last five years;
2. older editions that have not circulated in three years after a newer edition has been acquired, depending on discipline;

3. materials that contain obsolete or incorrect information and are not of historical value;
4. material that is damaged and cannot be repaired.

Specific Criteria for Retention are :

1. material that meets accreditation standards;
2. items identified by faculty, which should be retained regardless of the above-stated criteria for removal;
3. items considered valuable for the integrity of the collection by librarians.

(c) Procedure

1. Copyright date, imprint date or published date should be checked to find the age of the book.
2. The purchase date of the book (whichever is available) should be checked in order to find the length of time the book was owned by the library.
3. The last circulation date or check-out date should be checked to find the latest use, of items mentioned in number 1 and 2 of Specific Criteria for Consideration for Removal.
4. The table of contents of each book should carefully be examined in order to find the subject of the book and its relevance to the collection.
5. A final list of weeded books will be acquired from the Cataloguing Unit. A list of faculty members who participate in the weeding process will be sent to the Collection Development Librarian to be included in the Annual Report.
6. Weeding of the collection in one subject should be done on a yearly basis and preferably between spring / summer or summer/ fall breaks when institute is closed and there is less traffic in the book stack area. Department liaisons will receive a list of proposed books for withdrawal from the bibliographer.
7. In the event when a liaison or a faculty member does not respond to the list of books for potential withdrawal within the two-month time period, the head of the department will be notified and the deadline will be extended until the end of the semester. The Collection Development Librarian, Reference Librarian, and the Library Director will evaluate the processed titles for withdrawal if no word is received by any faculty member of that department. Any book requested by any of these individuals should be sent

back to Cataloguing unit to change the status and returned to the stacks.

(d) Discouraging Factors

Inspite of the compelling reasons for periodic weeding out documents from a library many librarians hesitate to put it in practice. It is quite evident in our country. The following are some of the reasons for such a version:

(i) Love for Numbers : The glory for numbers in libraries is still there. Though modern libranians realize that it is the quality of service that is more important than the quantity of documents in library even then they hesitate to weed out documents which are no longer useful. This is mainly because official reports to be submitted by them emphasize on numbers.

(ii) Sanctity of Collection : Many feel that very book however old it may has its value. Sometimes they think that antiquity enhances the value of the book even though it exact reprint in a better physical condition is available in the market. But in service library documents loose their value and significance if they got mixed up with large number of outdated and useless documents.

(iii) Pressure of Work : Library being a dynamic organisation, work pressure will always be on the library professionals. Since weeding implies careful, judicious and justifiable action, which needs time, librarians hesitate to weed out. Hindrance to or dislocation of the routine duties, due to time consumed by weeding out work, may not be appreciated by the clientele.

(v) Fear of Audit and Clientele Comments : At the time of audit one may face objection that documents for which amounts were paid are not found in the library. Similarly, the clientele may also comment upon the documents weeded out of the library saying that some very useful documents were also discarded.

But a librarian need not get discouraged by these factors. A clear and well planned weeding out policy free form bias and approved by a committee appointed either for this purpose of the one looking after the library affairs will clear all hurdles. Katz says that the weeding is one of the best suitable techniques available to ensure long range usefulness of any collection.

(e) What to do with Weeded Materials

The next problem is what to do when materials are to be weeded out on sound principles? Of course the materials that are withdrawn from the collection may be disposed of by any of the following methods, listed in priority order.

1. Items requested by faculty to be sent to their departments will be so marked and either picked up by faculty or sent through campus mail following withdrawal procedures. Cataloguing records will indicate that the numbers of materials were sent to the designated department (s).
2. Materials may be given to any non-profit organisations and will be so offered as deemed appropriate by the Collection Development Librarian, or faculty members.
3. Materials may be sold during the Library's Annual Book Sale.
4. Materials may be discarded if none of the above-stated options proves to be available.

Impact of IT Environment

In recent years, information technologies have advanced to such an extent that their impact on libraries is significant. Particularly, development regarding digital libraries, Internet, electronic publications, CD-ROMS, etc., have forced the librarians to change the way they are now functioning. In this context and also due to the budgetary constraints, librarians are giving importance to 'accessing the other libraries' collection' rather than 'possessing almost all documents' on a given subject. For instance, a number of full text databases are available on Internet. Why can't one access such records and download, if necessary? Once downloaded, such electronic documents, must be classified and catalogued, so that one need not search and download the same documents again, if and when required. In some cases, however, it may be economic to download again.

In conclusion, it can be said that the collection development is a decision making process, planned on the basis of objectives, scope, goals, programmes of the institution, needing cost effective and impartial implementation, and is the effective decision being taken by library staff, with the aid and advice of faculty. The challenge we to face is not a paperless society' nor the 'electronic information centre'. The challenge is to maintain, nurture and optimise the resources of the libraries with the help of new technology. Hence, we must be ready, emotionally, professionally and financially to accept and make good use of new technology.

2 (A)
Acquisition Section : Policy, Source and Work

Q. : Describe the chain works involved in the acquisition of books from publisher to library.

or

Describe the objectives and functions of acquisition section of a library.

Ans: To provide effective library services to its users the library has to acquire suitable reading material. The aim of the library is to select, procure, organize and disseminate information depending upon the need and requirement of its users. In present situation because of multidisciplinary nature of subject it is difficult for any library to buy all the published demand therefore, selection and procurement are crucial function of library. Library should try to build balanced collection of demands for its current and potential use.

Though objectives of library may vary depending upon their users requirements yet main aims of any library are :

(i) To fulfil the aim, objectives and goals of the organisation/ institution for which it has been established.

(ii) To encourage reading habits of the users.

(iii) To allow for all the people full access to books and other forms of recorded knowledge.

(iv) To preserve and communicate knowledge of the past and present to the present generation, as well as to the future generation.

Acquisition Policy

As books makeup a vital part of the stock of the library, acquisition is regarded as fundamental function of a library. It is necessary to have the acquisition policy formulated before actually indulging in the selection of books.

The Acquisition policy and procedures needed to fulfill the

(i) Aims and objectives of the organisation for which it has been established,

(ii) Financial limitations and

(iii) Type of services to be provided to the users.

Sources of Book-Selection

There are various sources used for selection of books in the library. They are:-

(i) Readers : Readers suggest either in written or verbally the books to be procured in the library. Sometimes, the readers suggestions prove very valuable in finding the gap in the collection or making the collection up-to-date.

(ii) Reviews: Scientific and technical periodicals, news papers, trade journals, having book review columns are important sources of book selection. The critical and evaluative reviews by subject experts and specialists are the best means for evaluating books. Scanning the reviewing periodicals regularly is a basic procedure in book selection.

(iii) Publishers catalogues.

(iv) List of new and recent publications issued by learned societies, universities, and other specialized bodies are of high informative value as a guide to the selection of books.

(v) Book exhibitions and;

(vi) Books sent by booksellers on approval basis also help greatly in the book selection and procurement of recently published books.

Book-Selection Tools

Book Selection tools/aids provides necessary information about books, their content, bibliographic details and physical formats. Due to unprecedented knowledge explosion, it is imperative for the books selector to become an expert in using selection tools. Some of the important tools/aids are :

(i) Books received from local vendors/booksellers on approval basis.

(ii) Reviews published in newspapers, and periodicals.

(iii) Users, subject, expert specialists, etc.

(iv) Publishers, booksellers, and other Book Traders Catalogues.

(v) Bibliographics such as Indian Books in Print, Indian National Bibliography, Cumutative Book Index : A word list of books in the English language, British National Bibliography, Books-in-print, ASLIB Book list etc.

(vi) Through Internet (*websites like www.amazon.com., www.booksbank.com* and *www.bookclubs.mcgraw-hill.com*)

Book-Selection

After selection, list is prepared and it is submitted to Book Selection Committee for the approval. To avoid duplication of books, each title should be checked from the library catalogue, list of ordered books, and list of books recently received in the library on approval.

The Book-Selection Committee will further Scrutinise and recommend for the approval by the Head of the Organisation. If some books are not approved, a separate list of Non-approved books is prepared and it is subsequently intimated to the indented user(s), and the Non-approved books, are returned to the venders/booksellers immediately, Format which may be used for by the librarian for making list of documents for approval given below:

Sr. No; Author's name(s), Title of document;

Publisher's name, International standard; Book Number; Year of Publication

Price in Indian/Foreign currency;

And demanded/indented by it User's name.

Book Order Section

The Book Selection and Evaluation is one of the most important functions of the library. However, equally important in the parallel operation in any library is Acquisition that is procuring documents after their selection. Every librarian needs some basics understanding and knowledge of how books are acquired for the library. There should be minimum delay in acquiring the document(s). There are various means of procuring a document in the library. Some of the important ones include :

(a) Purchase

(b) Gift

(c) Institutional membership

(d) Deposits

(e) Exchanges

(a) Purchase : Purchases form the major means of acquiring documents in any library. Strictly speaking, purchasing must be resorted to only when no other means is open to the library. But, most of the required items will not be available through other means and hence purchases against specific orders become the most usual practice in all libraries. Also because of this ordering procedure becomes a matter of major concern in document procurement.

(b) Gifts or Donations : Gifts or donations are always welcome in a library. There are many cases where personal collections bequeathed to libraries have become the main stay of collections. Such personal benefactions are to be explored and solicited by libraries. Gifts are possible also in the case of individual titles that are needed, particularly old and out-of-print books. Unsolicited gifts and gifts involving difficult terms and conditions need to be entertained with caution. Usefulness of the items should be the major deciding factor.

Unpriced publications that are distributed free make another important category in gifts. Timely knowledge and expedient action in acquiring them are important.

(c) Institutional Membership : Institutional membership is another potential resource in collection building. The library may enlist itself as a member of learned societies and institutions who publish useful materials. Often the membership subscription may cover the right to receive their publications either free of cost or at concessional prices.

(d) Deposit System: Deposit system entitles some specially designated libraries to receive free copies of the publications brought out by governments, national and international organisations, etc. There are many university libraries and state central libraries enjoying these benefits. There are also the national and state level libraries designated to receive free copies of all publications originated in India, either under provisions of the Copyright Law or the Delivery of Books and Newspapers (Public Libraries) Act, 1956. In all these cases the recipient library should be continuously on its alert about the new titles and their timely receipt.

(e) Exchanges : Exchanges may be another possible means of acquiring documents. In this case the recipient library or its parent body should have publications of its own to exchange with those of the other institutions. Exchanges are also possible between two libraries with spare copies against items needed.

Any how, the librarian depends primarily on the book booksellers and importers and sometimes publishers. In most cases, publishers do not supply books directly to the institutions and individuals. However, some publishers encourage direct suply to the libraries. The selection of vendors/booksellers should be made on the basis of their past services provided to library. The different practices followed by libraries in the choice of the supplier and effecting supplies are:

(a) Inquiry/Tender method

(b) Quotation method

(c) Standing Vendor method

(d) Books-on-approval method

(e) Open purchases

(f) Direct ordering with publishers

A library may adopt one or more of these methods. A brief description on each of them is given here:

(a) Inquiry/Tender Method : In Inquiry or Tender method, every book list of finally selected items is circulated among a number of booksellers who are invited to quote their lowest prices for each item. The order is placed for each item with the firm offering the lowest price.

(b) Quotation Method : In this method, quotations are invited for various categories of documents along with trade discounts admissible in each case, and the conversion rates in the case of foreign currency prices. This is done usually prior to the beginning of the financial year. The supplier for each category is fixed finally on the basis of the most economic terms offered.

(c) Standing Vendor Method : A Standing Vendor is one who is appointed as the authorised supplier to a library for a specified time, generally for a year or two, under prescribed terms and conditions of supply. The appointment is made on the basis of competitive quotations as in the Quotation method described earlier. But, in this case appointment will be based on expected total economy and efficiency rather than rates offered for separate categories.

(d) Books-on-Approval Method : Supply based on Book-on-Approval operates in two ways. In first case reputed publishers will be sending their new titles as and when published to the library directly. These items are accepted after due process of selection. The formal older will be placed with the local bookseller named by each publisher. If the book is not accepted it is returned to the same local bookseller. In the second ease, the local booksellers, at frequent intervals, bring some recent publications for approval and ordering. The selected items are included in a formal order and accepted while the others are returned. This method of Books-on-Approval is a common practice in most of the libraries.

(e) Open Purchase : Open purchase is possible when the library has decided about the terms and conditions of supply like the trade discounts and conversion rates. In this case documents can be bought from any bookseller who is agreeable to these terms, through as in shop selection, books-on-approval, or specific orders as the case may be.

Book fairs in major cities is a common occurrence now-a-days. Serveral publishers, both foreign and Indian including language books publishers take part in these fairs. It is a good opportunity to browse through and select good books.

(f) Direct Ordering with Publishers: Direct ordering with publishers or their representatives is adopted by some libraries. This has definite advantages in the case of foreign publications, provided the publishers have their representatives or wholesalers in the country. Even in this case of direct ordering, publishers and wholesalers usually channelize the supply only through the local dealers. Where a foreign publisher has no trade representation in the country, direct ordering will pose difficulties of import licenses and foreign exchange regulations.

Ordering Work

Once the Book Selection Committee's approval is obtained, supply order is placed to the appropriate vendor or publishers, To ensure prompt supply to books and efficient services, the library may frame up its additional terms and conditions, such as :

— **Preparation of Order Card :** The Card for these ordered books, should be prepared with the filed under "Books on order" in proper sequence immediately.

Relevant information such as Author, Title, Publishers, Edition, Price, ISBN, Name of the vendor/book seller etc. should be mentioned in the order card.

— **Intimation to the Indenters :** It is essential to inform the indenter(s)/user(s) about the action taken by the library for their indented or demanded books.

On receipt of book(s), before taking the book(s on charge, physical and general make-up of the book is checked and also the print quality, binding, maps, plates, floppy diskette(s), CD-disk(s) and other accompanying material should be checked.

Thereafter the book will be entered in the Accession register.

Accessioning Procedure

Accession Register is the basic record in the library about each document forming part of its collection. The general practice in libraries is to have a single register in which all types of documents whether purchased or received as gift or on exchange or as deposit are entered. But some libraries have the practice of using separate accession registers, for gifts and for deposited items. Still another practice is to have the accession list in card form. In this case, the card used at the stage of book selection will be converted into the accession card and filed in the accession number sequence and kept under safe custody.

The following jobs are involved in accessioning:

* Arranging the bills and the books in parallel sequence.
* Entering details in the Accession Register.
* Writing the Accession number on each book.
* Certifying the bills.
* Transmitting the bills for passing work.
* Transmitting the books for processing.
* Noting and filling the cards.

Documents are entered in the Accession Register date-wise according to their receipt in the library. All purchased books are entered in the order of the bills. For this purpose, the bills have to be first

ACCESSION REGISTER

Name of Library

Date	Acc. Number	Author	Title	Publisher & Place	Vol.	Edn.	Yr.	Pp.	Source/Bill No. & Date	Order No. & Date	Cost	Remarks

arranged in the ascending order of their dates. Books covered by each bill then have to be arranged and kept in the order in which they are listed in the bill. Book after book and bill after bill are then entered in the Accession Register keeping, the Accession Numbers running continuously. The Accession Number getting assigned to each document entered in the Accession Register will be a unique number which can identify that document. The Accession Number is then written legibly on the verso of the title page of the book and if necessary, on a clue page. The same number is then noted in the bill against the item. After entering all the items covered by one bill a certificate must be furnished on the bill which should read as :

> "certified that all the books as per the bill have been duly entered in the Accession Register vide numbers from......... to......................

The bills relating to the books accessioned are then handed over for Bill Passing Work while the books are sent to the Technical Department for processing. The cards belonging to them, after noting the date of accessioning and the Accession Numbers are filed in a tray labelled as "Books-In-Process".

Passing of Bills

The various jobs involved in the Bill Passing Work are:

* Checking
* Certifying
* Passing
* Transmitting

A serious risk involved in Bill Passing Work is either double payment or over-payment. Sufficient caution should be exercised to avoid both. Every bill should be carefully scrutinised by checking the calculations and totals, the conversion rates, and the trade discounts provided. In order to have uniformity in the procurement and to avoid fluctuations in conversion rates of foreign currencies, it is better to follow the norms givens by Good Office Committee (GOC). When verified and found correct a certificate to that effect should be furnished on each bill. This should read as:

> "Certified that the net published prices at the approved rates of conversion have been charged, and agreed rates of discounts have been allowed"

Flow Chart for Acquisition of Documents in Library

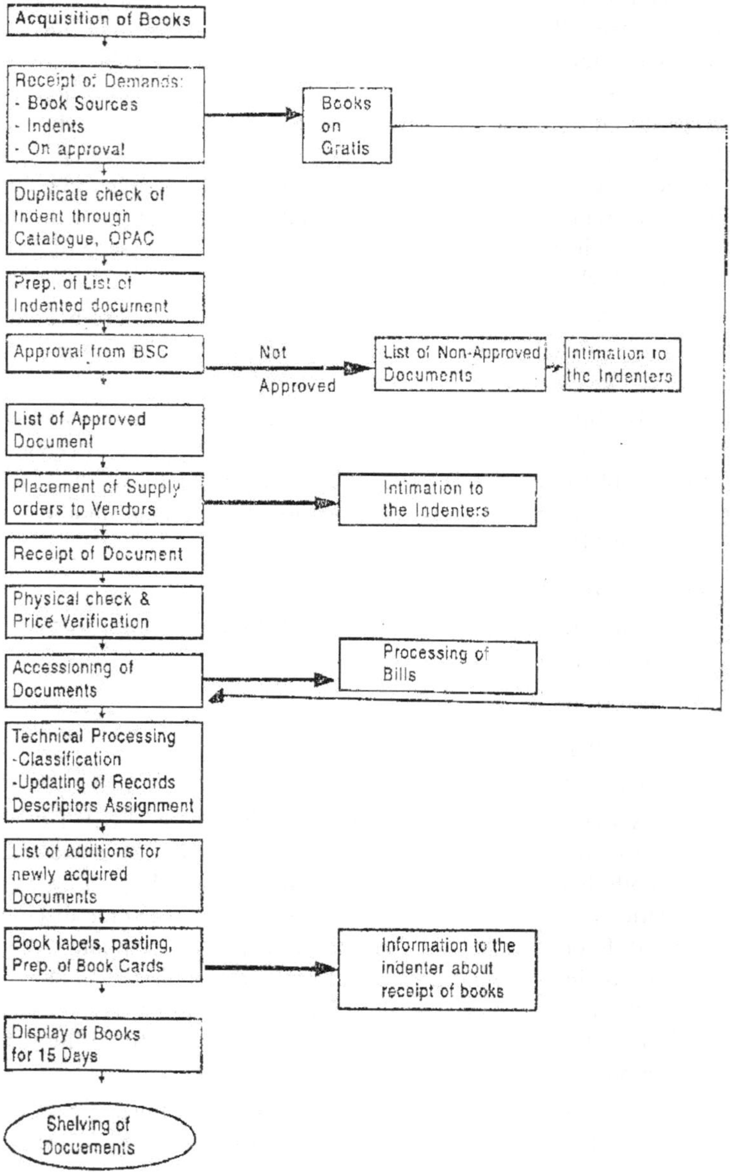

Each certified bill together with the Accession Register should be placed with the librarian for the final passing. He should satisfy himself after checking the bill and the corresponding entries in the Accession Register. He then should put his initials on the Accession Register and pass the bill for payment. This is done by writing at the bottom of the bill the words "Passed for payment" and putting his signature and office seal below. The passed bills are then transmitted to the Account Section for payment.

Thus, the accession work is completed in a library.

Q. : Name the different types of non-print materials and how they are selected and acquisioned in libraries?

or

Write an essay on selection, acquisition and organization of non-book/non-print materials in a library.

Ans. According to second edition of the Anglo-American Cataloguing Rules (AACR), Non-books materials include :

- sound recordings,
- video recordings, including interactive video discs;
- graphic materials - photographs, illustrations, postcards and slides;
- micro-computer software, including CD-ROM etc.

In addition, other forms covered by the term NBM are microforms - microfilms, microfiche, etc., models, wall charts, etc. As a matter of fact, microform dates back to the year 1839 when John Benjamin Dancer, an optician and professional photographer, produced the first micro-photograph. These microforms, perhaps, offer an alternative to book storage and help in solving the space problems encountered by libraries.

Basically, in a library, non-book materials come into two types. The first category is that where the main portion of the materials is non-book, but they may be accompanied by textual material in the form of a pamphlet or guide which would not be useful separated from the main portion. For example :

Music scores/part (unbound)

Computer disks

CD-ROMs

Laser disks

Videocassettes

Sound cassettes

Slides

Loose-leaf binders (selected)

Microforms accompanied by other non-book materials

Charts

Plates/photos

Second category include those materials which are created and originated independently such as videotapes, film strips, slide collections, pamphlets, news clippings files, and full text data files, and these should not be overlooked by the researcher as valuable information sources. Audio and visual materials often may be useful to add depth and additional interest to presentations. Pamphlets may succinctly cover many topics of current interest. News clippings files may include photos of current events of celebrities that may not be found easily elsewhere.

Additional non-book materials include databases, both online and on CD-ROM, and microform materials. Many periodicals are stored in microform to save shelf space. A periodical may be kept on microfilm or on microfiche. Microfilm is a continuous strip of film that is wound on a reel and viewed frame by frame. Microfiche is a single card that has images reproduced in rows and columns. Newspapers are typically stored on microfilm. Commenting on the value of NBM, it was said by Leslie Gillert and Jan Wright as early as in 1971 that :

"NBM have increased the range and means of obtaining and exploiting information for teaching, learning and research purposes, but to separate books from NBM is to divide information into false compartments. Hence, it is essential that books and non-books can be jointly identified and located to meet particular needs"

In spite of this recognition, NBM have not become popular in libraries due to the following reasons:

(i) A lack of understanding or only recent concern with the learning processes by university academics.

(ii) The strong belief in the primacy of the printed word for research collections.

(iii) Little demand from users, who, perhaps, were dominated by the conventional information resources and with little expcsure or access to NBM.

(iv) Lack of motivation and funds to build up NBM collecticns, etc.

Selection, Acquisition and Organisation of Non-Book/Non-Print Materials

Selection

1. **Authenticity :** Accurate Facts; facts impartially presented; up-to-date information; other acceptable works of Producer.
2. **Appropriateness:** Vocabulary at users levels; concepts at users level; useful data; media subject correlation (eg., Preprints to art, specimens to science) titles, captions etc. related to subject; narration, dialogue, sound effects related to subject; individual and/or group use suitability.
3. **Scope :** Small coverage as indicated; superior concept development by this means; Content to satisfy demands for current subjects.
4. **Interest:** Relationship to user's experience; intellectual challenge; curiosity satisfaction; credibility; imagination appeal; human appeal; sensory appeal.
5. **Organisation :** Logical developments; pertinence of all sequence; background elements; balance in the use of narration and dialogue.
6. **Technical aspects :** Tone fidelity; clarity; intelligibility; in-focus pictures; true size relationship; unified composition; effective colour use; complete synchronization of sound and image.
7. **Special Features:** Descriptive notes; teachers/users guide; permanent accompanying material.
8. **Physical characteristics:** Ease in handling for use and storage; minimum instruction for individual use; Attractive packing; during; durability; ease of repair.
9. **Library potential:** Relevancy that promotes communication; flexibility for many effective uses.
10. **Selection aids**: recommendation in evaluation sources and;
11. **Cost:** Conforming to budget; less expensive for satisfactory

substitutes average supplemental costs for replacement; repair; physical processing; storage.

Acquisition

For the most part, ordering non-book/non-print materials (microforms, films, videotapes, cassettee tapes, audio books, compact disks) is handled like book ordering. Some differences include; libraries often place orders directly with publishers rather than with vendors; preview copies are usually not new copies and are returned to the publisher regardless of whether an order is placed; requests for preview and purchases copies take more time to fulfill.

"Acquiring" digitized data requires consideration of several factors not found in other areas of acquisitions. Your decision to acquire - that is, to make available to your customers - online and CD-ROM resources will be driven by the library's ability to provide delivery platforms or gateways, the availability of user support and training, and by your community's interest in the many types of information available. Because electronic resources often require licensing agreements rather than true purchasing, "acquiring" these resources is a continuing process. The process may include comparing prices for print, electronic and combined print/electronic databases, choosing a flat fee or per-search fee structure, monitoring on-going charges and periodically reviewing the resource to ensure that it is meeting the needs of the community.

Organisation

The most important and effective actions that one can take care to organize these non-book materials are to create a stable environment and provide archival storage conditions. All of these items would benefit significantly if stored in a climate controlled environment. For these materials a type of Accession Register may be useful but additional columns for detailed information about the script, format, and other physical aspects should be provided which are not found in records of reading materials kept in book form. But it is advisable to maintain separate registers for non-book materials since their purpose, use, handling and location etc. will otherwise bring in so many difficulties. The utilitarians would prefer to keep the records of these non-book materials also on cards.

Q. : What are the general principles of book / non-book materials selection in a library? Describe some of the book-selection tools in details.

or

What are the various selection tools available in selecting the non-book/non-print materials in a library ?

Ans. From the earliest times when libraries became service institutions the policy of selecting documents was there. The reasons are (i) not every document is useful for a library (ii) it should satisfy the objectives of the library and (iii) even if a document is useful sometimes the amount needed for its acquisition may so high that the library cannot afford its acquisition.

So certain general principles are to be ensured for selection of documents. Drury has enuciated the following principles of book selection:

(i) Apportion the library funds in such a way as to obtain books of high quality for the greatest number of people.

(ii) Secure any book which the library can use with advantage.

(iii) Fix upon a policy of selection and stick to it until it has been proved wrong.

(iv) Select books that represent any endeavour aiming at human development, material, mental or moral.

Ranganathan suggested the following ideals for book selection.

(i) The ideal is to select only after inspection and perusal. Conform to this ideal whenever facilities exist for it, either in the form of the chief book centre being not far from the library or of booksellers or the agents for the publishers, taking the books from place to place.

(ii) Impeccable character and integrity should be brought to bear on the discharge of duties connected with book selection and assessment of potential wants of the readers free from any speaking tendency to please the whims and fancies of the members of the library committee.

(iii) Book selection should be the joint responsibility of the library staff and teaching staff. They should be guided by the probability of getting readers for the books selected. Book selection should never be vitiated by considerations of privilege.

(iv) Save the time of the staff by eliminating time lag in book selection. To eliminate time lag book selection may with due circumspection, base itself on the advance announcement of books by publishers of repute.

(v) Judge not hastily or light heartedly; reject not easily. Error on the side of selection rather than rejection.

Above principles are to be followed by a library for building up its collection.

(a) Book Selection Tools

Today, there are various type of aids available for better book selection. The most useful bibliographical aid indicating all books published, in India is the *Indian National Bibliography* first published in 1958, in United Kingdom, the '*British National Bibliography,* published since 1950 and in America the '*Cumulative Book Index*' published monthly the list of every book in English Language.

Journals are also useful to aid current book selection. Journals generally contain regular reviews of the books in the concerned subject. There are some aids, which are periodically published by book sellers and publishers, containing information on the available books and also forthcoming books. However, following bibliographical tools are more useful in book selection.

(i) Books published in America (U.S.A.)

1. American Book Published Record, New York, R.R. Bowker, Monthly.

The entries are arranged according to classified order by Dewey Decimal classification schemes. It includes all the entries of four issues of the 'weekly record' section of the publisher's weekly. It is also cumulated annually in a classified order. Author and title indexes are provided.

2. A Reader's Guide and Bookman's manual: A guide to literature. New York, R.R.Bowker, 1960.

3. Books in Print. New York, R.R.Bowker, 1948———Annual.

It gives details about the books published in U.S.A. in a limited time period, in which the entries of publisher's trade list are rearranged under author, title and series sequences. Now it is published in two volumes. In Vol. I- entries are arranged by author and editor and in Vol. 2-entries are arranged by titles and series.

4. Book list and subscription books bulletin, Chicago, American library association, 1905 - Fortnightly, (monthly in August).

It gives the information of the selected books as recommended by the ALA for public libraries, in which entries are arranged by classified order of Dewey Decimal Classification scheme. An author and subject index is also introduced. However an annual index for author, title, imprint, series is also available. (In 1956, the subscription books bulletin was merged with the book list).

5. *Book Review Digest.* New York, H.W. Wilson, 1905, Monthly (Except in February and July)

It lists more than 4,000 book reviews, published in 70 English and American journals. The entries of books are arranged alphabetically by author's name, with separate title and subject index. It gives the complete information of the book alongwith annotation. The half yearly and five-yearly cumulative volumes are also available.

6. *Cumulative Book Index :* World list of Scientific Books of English languages. New York, H. W. Wilson, 1898 - Monthly (Except July, August and December).

It includes all the books of world published in English language, except government publications, pamphlets and ephemera and entries are arranged alphabetically by subject, author, collaborators, title, series in one sequence. Each entry gives the detailed information of the book alongwith Library of Congress card number. It is also cumulated into half-yearly and two yearly volumes.

7. Library of Congress Catalogue, Book, Subject, Washington. Library of Congress, 1950 - , Quarterly.

It includes the books recently published and also available in the annual and quinquennial cumulative volumes. The entries are arranged alphabetically by subject.

8. Library Journal, New York, R.R. Bowker, 1878, Fortnightly (Monthly in July and August).

It publishes the annotation list of various useful books for libraries and also a list of childern's books. The entries are arranged alphabetically by subject.

9. National Union Catalogue, Washingtion, Library of Congress, 1948 - (Monthly).

It includes the books received in the Library of Congress, excluding books of the National Library of Medicine Catalogue and the bibliography of Agriculture. The entries are alphabetically arranged by author and cumulated into quarterly and annual volumes.

10. Publishers Trade List Annual, New York, R.R. Bowker, 1879-, (Annual).

It publishes the trade lists of numerous publishers of America.The entries are arranged alphabetically by author.

11. Publisher's Weekly, New York,, R.R.Bowker, 1872 -

It includes the new books of the week published in U.S.A. and each entry provides detailed information with annotation. The entries are arranged in alphabetical order by author. It is monthly cumulated as a title index.

12. Scientific, Medical and Technical books, edited by R.R.Hawkings 2nd ed. Washington, National Academy of Sciences, National Research Council, 1958.

It includes selected books published in America on scientific, medical and technical subjects.

13. Subject Guide to Books in Print. New York, R.R. Bowker. 1950 - Annual.

It publishes information of the American books in print. Each entry gives bibliographical details and entries are arranged in alphabetical order by subject.

(ii) Books Published in Great Britain

1. ASLIB Book List. London, ASLIB, 1935 - Monthly.

It published a monthly list of more than 70 recommended books on scientific and technical subjects. Each entry gives the detailed bibliographical information along with annotation. The entries are arranged in a classified order by U.D.C. in four parts; Elementary, Intermediate. Advanced and Reference Books.

2. Book-seller, London J. Whitaker and Sons, 1858 - 1908, Monthly; 1909 - Weekly.

It covers all the published British books of each subject. Each entry gives full bibliographical details and is arranged in an alphabetical order. It has monthly, quarterly and yearly cumulations.

3. British Books in Print : The Reference Catalogue of Current Literature, London, Whitaker, 1887 - Irregular, Annual.

It was previously known as 'Reference Catalogue of Current Literature, but now it is called 'British Books in Print'. It contains information on about 2,00,000 British books, which are in prints and available at a particular time from about 3,000 British book-sellers. It has two volumes as under :

Vol. 1 - Author Index, i.e., author, editor, and other collaborators.

Vol. 2 - Title index, i.e., Title and subject forming part of the title.

4. British Book News, London, British Council, 1904 - Monthly,

It publishes 250 important selective books published in U.K. and Commonwealth, each month. The entries are arranged in classified order.

5. British National Bibliography, London, Council of British National Bibliography, 1950 - Weekly.

It publishes the British publications received at the British Museum of a week under Copyright Act. Dewey Decimal Classification scheme is followed for arrangement of the entries. The alphabetical indexes of a author and title are also provided. The entries are catalogued according to the A.A. code. The cumulation of author index is published every month. BNB has monthly, quarterly yearly and quinquennial cumulations.

6. Times Literary Supplement. London, The Times (Daily News paper), 1902 - Weekly.

It reviews British Books on humanities and social sciences by subject specialists.

7. Whitaker's Cumulative Index. London, Whitaker, 1924 - Quarterly and Annual.

It contains all British Boooks published during the quarter period. Each entry gives bibliographical details and class number according to the Dewey Decimal Classification scheme. The entries are arranged in the classified orfer and alphabetically by subject. The author and title indexes are available separately. Annual cumulation is also available.

(iii) Books published in India

(a) English Books

1. Documentation on Asia, edited by Girija Kumar and V. Machwe. New Delhi, Allied Publishers, 1963 - Vol. I - 1960 - Annual.

It publishes a Bibliography of current literature on Asia, in which the entries are arranged according to the geographical areas and subarranged according to subjects.

2. Indian National Bibliography, Calcutta, Central Reference Library, National Library, 1957 -. Quarterly, 1964 - Monthly.

It contains all books in English and Indian languages, received in the National library under the *Delivery of Books and Newspapers Act 1954* (as amended in 1956). This bibliography has two parts. Further, each part is bifurcated as:

(i) Classified section, and

(ii) Alphabetical section. The monthly issues are cumulated into annual volumes.

3. Indian Books in Print, complied by Sher Singh and S.N.Sandhu. Delhi, Indian Bureau of Bibliographies, 1981.

It contains details of English books and imprint in India. Each entry includes the bibliographical details along with price.

4. The National Bibliography of Indian Literature, New Delhi. Sahitya Academy, 1962 -

It includes all Indian books of literary merit and abiding value, in four Indian languages, Assamese, Bengali, English and Gujarati, published in India in four separate volumes. The entries have bibliographical details in Roman script with an annotation in English language.

5. Indian Press Index, with Book Review Supplement, April, 1968 —.

It contains the bibliography of the books reviewed in newspapers indexed in the Indian Press Index.

6. Indian Scientific and Technical Publications; A bibliography complied by National library. Council of Scientific and Industrial Research, New Delhi.

It is a selected bibliography of scientific and technical books in

English and other Indian languages published in India. The entries are arranged in a classified order in two parts.

Part I. Indian languages, published work.

Part II. English Books.

7. Impex Reference Catalogue of Indian Books, New Delhi. Indian Book Export and Import Co. 1960 -

It is a comprehensive list of valuable books published and printed in India. The entries are arranged in two sections.

Section. I - Under broad alphabetical subject groups.

Section II - Under author, title, catchwords title and series.

8. Publisher's catalogues.

Several publishers publish the periodical catalogue of their publications. Shree Publishing Books catalogue by M/s Shree Publishing Delhi, Book News by Jain Book Depot, Publishers monthly by M/s. Chand & Co. (Delhi), Asia Bulletin by M/s. Asia Publishing House (Mumbai) monthly, Oxford University Press Catalogue by M/s Oxford University Press, New Delhi and Library Refresher by Ess Ess Publications, New Delhi are some of the examples.

9. Bookseller's 'Catalogues

These are published by many big or small booksellers, for the books available in their stock e.g. UBS's catalogues, Indian Book House's catalogue, Shivalal Agrawal's catalogue and Bishen Singh Mahendra Pal Singh, Dehradun etc.

(b) Tools for Non-Book/Non-print Materials

The use of non-print information materials in libraries have become more popular and it can be possible only if the library acquires the necessary and appropriate equipment. Selection of equipment also is as important as selecting and collection of non-print materials. There are two important factors in the selection : (1) standardisation and (2) changing media field. These two factors combine to make equipment buying too hazardous to risk collection of non-book/non-print materials. However, this aspect is given the greatest attention by all concerned, nationally and internationally. Some of the tools that might help selection of equipment are listed below:

Sound Recordings	*National Sounds Archive's Directory of Recorded Sound Resources in the United Kingdom.*
Video Recordings	*British National Film and Video Catalogue (BNFVC); British Universities Film and Video Council Catalogue (BuFVC Catalogue); the Video Gallery; Educational Film/ Video Locator Lists; Library Video Magazine, etc.*
Videodiscs	*International Bildplatten Katalogue; the Videodisc monitor; Interactive update.*
Graphics	*Illustrations Index.*
Microcomputing Software	*Directory of Hardware and Directory of Software (National Computing Centre); Personal Computer World; Educational Computing; the Computer Users Yearbook and Software Users Handbook.*
CD-ROM	*CD-ROM Directory; CIMTTICH; Library and information Briefings (from Central London Polytechnic Library and Information Technology Centre, Publishers, Catalogues (Silver Plater, Multi-lingual, UMI etc.*

2 (B)
Technical Section Work

Q. : Describe the functions of Technical Section of a library.

Ans. : One of the important sections in a library is the Technical Section as it occupies a pivotal position round which all other activities take place. It is called by other names, such as, Processing Department, Technical Processing Section, Cataloguing Department, Technical Department, etc. Irrespective of the name by which it is called, the objective and functions of this section remain the same. While the acquisition is responsible for the building up of a good collection, it is the Technical Section that transforms the collection of documents into serviceable units. Thus, it achieves mainly by performing two functions, namely, technical processing which includes classification and cataloguing, and physical preparation of the documents for circulation and use by the readers.

Need for Technical Processing

The need for technical processing has been brought about by a number of reasons/factors. They are:

(i) Accelerated growth of information resulting in the production of a large number of documents and, consequently, user problems of inadequate time for reading and assimilation.

(ii) Complexity in subject specialisation coupled with the interdisciplinary nature of information.

(iii) Demand from readers for better services, etc.

The main functions of Technical sections are

* Classification and
* Cataloguing

CLASSIFICATION

Classification is the foundation of librarianship. Classification, in common parlance, means arrangement. To state it more clearly, it means 'to bring order out of chaos'. The library partakes the nature of a growing organism. It presents problems of such an enormous growth that compels librarians to thick of devising certain methods by which they can bring order out of chaos and can maintain it. The same books are used time after again. It mean that if a permanent order is not brought in, the time spent in arranging, dearranging and rearranging will be so much that the readers will become sore about the libraries and they will begin to detest the library service. In this way the purpose of libraries will be lost. In order to vouchsafe a permanent arrangement, librarians have invented many classification schemes. All these schemes have their own merits and demerits and have got universal applicability but may not suit all conditions at all times in all places. Therefore, while deciding the adoption of a particular classification scheme, one should take into consideration various merits and demerits of all such schemes and their applicability to the book stocks of a particular library. The following are the important classification schemes which are used in various libraries of the world.

1. Dewey Decimal Classification by Melvil Dewey
2. Universal Decimal Classification
3. Library of Congress Classification
4. Subject Classification by J.D.Brown
5. Expansive Classification by C.A. Cutter
6. Bibliographic Classification by H.E.Bliss
7. Colon Classification by Dr. S.R.Ranganathan
8. Rider's International Classification by Fremont Rider

All these schemes of classification except Colon Classification Scheme are of foreign origin and have got bias towards Western subject. Eastern subjects have been ignored to a great extent. Moreover, almost all these schemes are enumerative schemes. Bibliographic and Colon Classification schemes are analytico-synthetic schemes. Out of all these schemes, Dewey Decimal Classification scheme is widely used in all the countries of the world including India.

Tools for Classification

The schedules of the classification scheme used in a particular library are the major tools of the classifier. In order to interpret the schedules of a particular scheme, other aids as given below can also be helpful for ensuring uniform class numbers for particular books-

1. Code for Classifiers by W.S.Merrill, 1939.
2. Indian National Bibliography 1957—.
3. British National Bibliography, 1950—.
4. Library of Congress Catalogue 1898—.
5. The National Union Catalogue (U.S.), 1948—.
6. American Book Publishing Record 1906—.

The classifiers can rely safely upon the above-mentioned standard tools because expert classifiers are responsible for classifying the books listed in these bibliographies and catalogues. It would be economical if class numbers are taken directly from these tools.

Classification procedure

After receiving the books from the Order Section after accessioning, the following jobs are performed for classifying the books:

(i) Duplicate checking.

(ii) Determining specific subject of the book.

(iii) Allotting class number by referring to the Classification schedules.

(iv) Assigning Book Numbers.

(v) Assigning Subject Headings.

(vi) Checking of class numbers and subject headings by the Chief Classifier.

(vii) Maintenance of staff manual.

(i) Duplicate checking : In big libraries, duplicate checking is the job of the Order Section. The Assistant of the said section gives the requisite information on the book selection cards which are ultimately sent to the Processing Section alongwith the books. As such the labour of the Classification Section is saved. All the same, in those libraries where this system is not in vogue, the under mentioned procedures are followed for duplicate checking:

(a) All the books are divided into two main groups, i.e., fiction and nonfiction. The later group is further divided into various sub-group representing various subject.

(b) Books in each group/subject are arranged alphabetically by author.

(c) These books are taken to the public catalogue for checking, if official catalogue is not maintained.

(d) The Assistant first checks the books with the main entry/ author entry. If many title cards representing same author are found in the catalogue, then edition and year of publication are checked. In case of doubt, other entries are also checked. For pseudonymous authors, cards giving their real names are also looked for.

(e) The word 'Add' is written in pencil on the fly leaf of those books for which the catalogue cards are found in catalogue. Call numbers for these books are written on the verso of the title pages.

(f) The words "Main & Shelf" or letters "M & S" are written in pencil on the fly leaf of those books of which earlier editions are available in the library catalogue.

(g) The remaining books are taken back to the classifier for classifying.

(ii) Determining the specific subject : The books, the cards for which are not found in the catalogue, are taken over by the classifiers. They, first of all, find out the specific subject of each book by going through the following parts of the book in a successive manner :

1. Title
2. Sub-title
3. Foreword
4. Preface
5. Table of Contents
6. Book Jacket's flaps
7. The Thought Content
8. Book Reviews

Generally, the specific subject can be found out by reading the title of a book but in cases where the specific subject is not clear from the title because of its misleading nature, the other parts of the book as given above are gone through.

(iii) Allotting class numbers : After determining the specific subject of each book, the classification schedules and other aids are used for allotting proper class numbers. The indexes attached to the classification schedules are also used to find out the class numbers, though complete reliance on the indexes is not advisable. In case of analytico-synthetic schemes, subjects are broken into various parts and the formulae for constructing Class Numbers are used for arriving at the exact class numbers.

Each library should make a policy decision as to whether close or broad classification is to be practised in the library otherwise there will be lot of confusion and inconsistency, especially in arrangement of books on the shelves. In general and small libraries, broad classification may be followed but in large academic, research and special libraries, close classification is desirable.

The Class Numbers so arrived at, should be tallied with the other standard catalogues, if necessity arises, especially in doubtful cases. The Class Numbers are given in pencil on the upper half portion of the verso of the title page. It is given in pencil, because in case there is some change in the Class Numbers in future it may be corrected without any damage to the book by rubbing the earlier Class Numbers. This phenomenon is common because almost every classification scheme is revised periodically.

(iv) Assigning Book Numbers : After allotting the Class Numbers, the classifier assigns the Book Numbers. The following are the systems of allotting Book Numbers:

1. Cutter's Author Table
2. Cutter-Sanborne Author Table
3. Merrill's Author Table
4. Author Tables of L. Stanley Jast
5. Biscoe Time Numbers
6. Ranganathan's Book Numbers System

Generally, author marks constitute a Book Number. Cutter's Table or Cutter-Sanborne Tables are generally used to allot author marks. Suppose the Book Number for the book 'An Introduction to Library Classification' by W.C. Berwick Sayers is to be allotted By using the Cutter - Sanborne Table, the book Number will be S 274 I. By analysing it, we find that 'S' is the first letter of the surname, 274 is the number given by Cutter - Sanborne Tale for representing Sayers, and 'I' stands for the first letter of the first word of the title of the book *i.e.* Introduction.

But in case of Colon Classification, Book Numbers consist of language, form, year of publication, accession part no., volume no., supplement no., copy no., etc. but the year of publication is sufficient for most of the general books. For example, the Book Number is to be allotted for a book published in 1994, the Book Number will be N 94. N stands for 1900 and 94 for the actual year number. A decision is to be taken by each library as to which system is to be used for allotting book numbers.

(v) Assigning subject headings : Subject headings are assigned by the classifier so that the cataloguer may prepare catalogue cards for the same. A classifier is in a better position to assign subject headings because be knows the subject of the book minutely. For assigning subject headings, the following tools may be used:-

1. Library of Congress List of Subject Headings.
2. Sears List of Subject Headings.
3. A.L.A. List of Subject Headings.
4. Ranganathan's Chain Procedure.

Out of the above-memtioned tools, the Chain Procedure method is most scientific and comprehensive one for deriving proper subject headings. It has been demonstrated by the British National Bibliography by its application. This system has been used generally by those libraries which are using Colon Classification and Classified Catalogue Code of Dr. Ranganathan. In this system, subject headings are derived by analysing the Class Numbers with the help of the classification scheme in use.

Those libraries, especially smaller ones, which do not make use of the Chain Procedure, may use the Sears List of Subject Headings or A.L.A. List of Subject Headings because in these libraries minute subject headings may not be required. But large, research or special libraries may use the Library of Congress List of Subject Headings which is a very comprehensive and standard one. But each library due to some local and special conditions has to adopt certain subject headings of its own in order to meet readers' demands.

On the back fly leaf of the book, the classifier writes down in pencil the subject headings. He gives other directions also *i.e.,* whether main and shelf cards are to be prepared or cards for joint authors, series etc. are to be made.

(vi) Checking by chief classifier : If there are more than one classifier, as they are bound to be in bigger libraries, the classification work of the juniors must be checked by the Chief Classifier, so that consistency is ensured. Otherwise there will be chaos and the-very purpose of classification will be defeated. After the Chief Classifier checks class numbers etc, the relevant books are sent on to the Cataloguing Department.

(vii) Maintenance of staff manual : If some modifications are effected in the schedules of classification scheme in use, these decisions should be properly recorded in a staff manual so that in case the classifiers leave the library or they are otherwise transferred to other departments of the library, the newcomers do not feel handicapped due to lack of proper guidance. The modifications, as already pointed out, should be decided in staff meetings after great thought and prolonged discussion so that wrong and hasty decisions are avoided. Such wrong decisions paralyse the whole system because it becomes very difficult to retrace the steps as the number of books to be reclassified and recatalogued becomes very large.

CATALOGUING

Classification determines the place of a book on the shelves. Physically, book can be placed only at one place according to the subject contents of the book, but the readers seek book through various approaches such as author, title, series, and other collaborators like translators, editors, etc. Classification is not capable of fulfilling these approaches of the readers. The catalogue comes to the rescue of the readers. It is needless to emphasize the importance of a catalogue because without it the whole purpose of libraries will be lost and most of the principles of library science evolved by Ranganathan will be violated. The book will not be put to much use.

Cataloguing Tools

The Cataloguing Department needs various tools for effective and correct cataloguing. These tools include the Cataloguing Code in use and various important biographical dictionaries, dictionaries of names and dates besides the following :—

1. Indian National Bibliography.
2. British National Bibliography.
3. Library of Congress Catalogue/National Union Catalogue.
4. American Book Publishing Record etc.

Cataloguing procedure

The cataloguing of books is an cumbersome job. It must be planned intelligently if it has to serve its purpose. Proper job analysis should be done and only those persons who can put their heart and soul into this work should be entrusted with this job. The following are the jobs which are involved in the Cataloguing Department:-

(i) Preparation of the Main Entry.
(ii) Preparation of Shelf list.
(iii) Preparation of Added and Reference entries.
(iv) Label pasting.
(v) Label writing and assigning location marks.
(vi) Checking of the catalogue cards by the Chief Cataloguer.
(vii) Alphabetization of Cards.
(viii) Card filing.
(ix) Cataloguing Updating work
(x) Releasing work

(i) Preparation of the Main Entry: In accordance with the rules of the cataloguing code in use, one of the cataloguers prepares the main entry card. This main entry card contains maximum information about the book. On the back of this card, tracing is done in pencil so that it can be changed without any damage to the card. By writing it on the back of the card, the readers are also saved from unnecessary confusion. This tracing provides guidance to the junior cataloguers as to how many and which added and reference entries are to be prepared. It is also useful at the time of withdrawing the cards of a book which is either lost or otherwise withdrawn from the stock of the library.

(ii) Preparation of Shelf List: A Shelf List Card is a duplicate copy of the Main entry card. For each book, one shelf list card is prepared.

(iii) Preparation of Added and Reference Entries : Division of labour and specialization of work are the order of the day. By specialization, quantity and quality of the work are improved. So is the case with the library work. Moreover, preparation of a main entry is a responsible job and the other added entries are merely duplication of the main entry with minor alterations and/or deletions etc. so it is better if this repetitive job is assigned to junior staff members. The tracings given on the back of the main entry card provide instructions to the juniors for preparing added and reference entries without any difficulty.

In case Unit Card method is followed, headings of various added entries are to be added on the top of the main entry card, many copies of which are received in typed/printed form in the library. Suppose, a title entry is to be prepared according to the Unit Card method. One copy of the main entry card is taken and the title is added on the top of this card. Thus, the title entry card is ready.

In case, Unit Card method is not followed, the added entries contain briefer information than that of the main entry card and these are prepared on blank lined cards separately.

(iv) Label Pasting: After the preparation of all the catalogue cards, the books are handed over to semi-professionals or unskilled workers who paste the labels in the books. The following labels are generally pasted in the books:-

1. **Spine Label :** Gummed white cloth is cut into round or square pieces of about 1.25" each. This label is pasted one inch above the bottom of the spine of the book. This is done so that the Call Number may be properly visible to the readers when the book is shelved in a book rack. Symmetrical arrangement can also be ensured. If the width of the book is much less and the spine label cannot be pasted on the spine, it should be pasted at the same level on the front card board. The specimen is given below:

Class No. Book No.

Class No. Book No.

2. Ownership Slip/Mark

(a) One Ownership Slip is generally pasted on the inner side of the front card board at left hand top most corner. The size of this slip may be about 3" × 2.5". The slip may be made of glazed paper. The specimen of the slip is given below:-

Name of the library Class No. Book no. Acc. No.

Ownership Slip

(b) Other ownership marks are put at various places of the book by rubber stamps or embossing machines. A stamp, which contains the name of the library is put on the title page and another on the secret page, to be decided by each library. Third stamp may be put at the end of the book. Its specimen is given as under :

Name of the Library Location Place

Ownership Stamp

3 Date Slip: One date slip is pasted on the top most portion of the front or back fly-leaf of each book. But for reference books, manuscripts and other books which are not to be issued, this slip is not pasted, otherwise this would be a wastage of time energy and stationery. The size of the said slip may be 5" × 3". Its specimen is given below:

2 (B)
Technical Section Work

Q. : Describe the functions of Technical Section of a library.

Ans. : One of the important sections in a library is the Technical Section as it occupies a pivotal position round which all other activities take place. It is called by other names, such as, Processing Department, Technical Processing Section, Cataloguing Department, Technical Department, etc. Irrespective of the name by which it is called, the objective and functions of this section remain the same. While the acquisition is responsible for the building up of a good collection, it is the Technical Section that transforms the collection of documents into serviceable units. Thus, it achieves mainly by performing two functions, namely, technical processing which includes classification and cataloguing, and physical preparation of the documents for circulation and use by the readers.

Need for Technical Processing

The need for technical processing has been brought about by a number of reasons/factors. They are:

(i) Accelerated growth of information resulting in the production of a large number of documents and, consequently, user problems of inadequate time for reading and assimilation.

(ii) Complexity in subject specialisation coupled with the interdisciplinary nature of information.

(iii) Demand from readers for better services, etc.

The main functions of Technical sections are

* Classification and
* Cataloguing

CLASSIFICATION

Classification is the foundation of librarianship. Classification,

<table>
<tr><td colspan="4">Call No. Acc. No.
Name of the Library
Author ....
Title ....</td></tr>
<tr><td colspan="4">This book was issued/is due on the date
last stamped or marked</td></tr>
<tr><td></td><td></td><td></td><td></td></tr>
</table>

Book Card

The size and shape of the book card may be reduced and changed in form in case Browne Charging System is to be followed, because in that system, no issue or return dates are marked on the Book Card. Its specimen is given below:

<table>
<tr><td>Name of the Library
Call ....
Acc. No. ....
Authors ....
Title ....</td></tr>
<tr><td></td></tr>
</table>

Book Card

(v) Label Writing and Assigning Location Marks : The pasted labels are written with pen but Computer printout can also be used. Junior staff members are deputed for this repetitive job. But this job is a very important one because if the labels are not accurately written, the book is likely to be misplaced. So the employees who are entrusted with this job should have a good handwriting and should be accurate enough. The *spine labels* contain the Call Number and the location mark of the book. These are written on the left-hand upper portion of the label. Such marks may be either Reference, Rare, Text Book, Reports etc. These words are abbreviated and followed consistently. Their specimens are given below :

Rare	R	RR
025	025	025
W 563 P	W 563 P	W 563 P
For a Rare Book	For a Reference Book	For a Report used as a Reference Book

Location Marks

(vi) Catalogue Cards checking by Chief Cataloguer : All the cards alongwith the catalogued books are submitted to the Chief Cataloguer for scrutiny and checking. In case of mistakes, the assistants are asked to correct the same. The Chief Cataloguer finds out as to whether all the cards have been properly made or not. Similarly, he has to satisfy himself to the effect that the label writing is done in an impersonal handwriting. It is better if the books are sent to the Librarian or other senior staff member for further checking. The books are thus, ready to be shelved and the catalogue cards are ready to be filed in the catalogue and shelf list cabinets.

(vii) Alphabetization of Cards : The catalogue cards to be filed in the public catalogue are alphabetized. For alphabetizing, there are two accepted methods *i.e.*, word by word or letter by letter. In accordance with the practice of the library, these cards are alphabetized by junior staff members. The shelf list cards are arranged in a classified order. It is desirable that the persons deputed for this work should not be transferred very often, otherwise there will be chaos. But in order to avoid indispensability, many persons should be trained in this art.

(viii) Card Filing Work : After the Accession List is made, the catalogue cards relating to the released documents are ready for merging with the catalogue. In the case of the Classified Catalogue, the Main Entries and the Cross Reference Entries are to be filed in its Classified Part while all the other Added Entries are to be filed in the Alphabetical Part. Since there is no classified part in the dictionary catalogue, all the entries are filed in a single alphabetical sequence. There are prescribed rules for filing. In the classified part of the Classified Catalogue, the ordinal values given to the various symbols in the Call Number will take care of this arrangement. Compared to this, the alphabetical arrangement appear to be easier. There are many cases in alphabetical filing where definite rules are needed for ensuring consistent in arrangement. Therefore, the library should have formulated rules of alphabetisation of its own, or have adopted some of the standard rules available, like the *A.L.A. Rules for Filing,* or the I.S.I. Standards for alphabetical arrangement. The Shelf-list Cards are filed in the Shelf-list.

(ix) Catalogue Updating Work: The updating and maintenance of the library catalogue is the sole responsibility of the Technical Department. This includes, besides the filing of the entries relating to the newly processed documents, occasional work of corrections, consolidations and withdrawals. Labelling the catalogue trays and providing adequate Guide Cards inside the trays are also to be attended to. Since the catalogue will be growing corresponding to the growth of the collection there will be a continuous need for the movement of the cards from one tray to another. Parallel to this movement, the labels and guide cards also will have to be moved.

(x) Releasing Work : Documents whose physical and technical processing have been completed are released for use at prescribed intervals, like once a week, once a fortnight, or once a month, etc. Releasing work also includes making lists of new additions or Accession List. For this purpose the Main Entries relating to the released documents are arranged in a classified order and sent for typing out the Accession List. The practice may vary from library to library with regard to the dissemination of information regarding new additions.

The Accession List may be put up on the Notice Board, printed or cyclostyled and copies mailed to members, or published in the weekly editions of newspapers, etc. The documents released at a time are usually placed on display for a week or so before they are merged in the general collection.

2(C)
Circulation Section : Work and Membership

Q. : What do you mean by Charging System? Describe any one charging system, explaining its merits and demerits.

or

What are the basic essential qualities of a good charging and discharging system? Discuss any charging and discharging system that fulfils these qualities.

or

Name the different charging and discharging systems. Describe the operation of Browne Charging System highlighting its advantages and disadvantages.

or

Bring out the difference between Browne charging system and Newark charging system.

Ans. Library documents are usually issued for home reading. The work of circulation has therefore to be planned and managed with efficiency. To check and control the movement of documents, it is necessary to have a system for the same. A circulation system helps a library user in the use of books and other library material that have been sent by the technical processing division of the library to the maintenance division most effectively. All jobs related to a method of borrowing books and returning them after use, creation and maintenance of relevant records and files etc. are referred to as circulation work.

The objectives of circulation service are:

(i) To maximize the availability of all library materials to users and thereby optimize their use;

(ii) Adopting effective charging and discharging systems and procedures of lending for all types of users with reference to the different types of documents; and

(iii) To develop means and mechanisms for the generation and maintenance of records.

Most often circulation work includes:

1. Registration of members
2. Lending of documents
3. Charging of overdues
4. Reservation of books
5. Renewal of books
6. Maintenance of records
7. Maintenance of Statistics
8. Inter Library Loan
9. Miscellancous Jobs

1. Member's Registration

First step in any circulation system is to register the patrons. This is a time consuming but necessary job for several reasons. Registration identifies the borrower as a member of community or as an enrolled student, faculty of staff members. In registration the name of user, address, telephone and other information is noted down with the signature of user.

The registration enables the members to take advantage of the privileges of the library.

2. Lending of Books

Circulation is an activity whereby library materials are lent to borrowers and records of such loans are maintained. It is this service that brings user into direct contact with an operating system of the library. Lending is related to charging and discharging. Good charging systems have following capability. It should be able to identify:

(i) The books are charged.

(j) Identify the borrowers who taken those books.

(k) Identify when a book is to be back in library.

(l) Measure the extent use of books.

(m) Indicate the number of books circulated per day.

3. Overdue Charges

It is general practice in libraries to collect overdue charges/fines for book returned after the due date. This policy is measure of control over proper use of books. This also results in instilling discipline. The amount of fines is varies and depend on library to library.

4. Reservation of Books

It is also known as hold procedure. This involved the procedure by which borrowed library materials are identified and reserved upon request by their users. In academic library, text books and other related material are in great demand, but library cannot purchase multiple copies due to budget problem. The solution is reservation of books by readers one by one.

5. Renewal of Books

Some books are required by readers for longer period for various reasons. Renewal represents the extension of the loan-period by recharging the same item to same person. Books may be renewed, if there is no demand for the same book. Renewal is based on the condition that the books will be returned immediately if recalled. Books may be renewed by presenting the book in person or by telephone or depending upon the policy of library.

6. Maintenance of Records

Maintenance of circulation record is very important because these become the sound basis for preparing various comparative statements. These serve as a reliable source for drawing a conclusion and comparison of the service of the library with those of others.

7. Maintenance of Statistics

The statistics are prepared on the basis of circulation records. The records are important because without these reliable records, Statistics cannot be prepared and annual report presented without these statistics will be incomplete.

8. Inter-Library Loan

As it is neither desirable nor feasible for a library to be totally self-sufficient, they need to depend on other cooperating libraries in the city or region, to obtain books and other library materials required by the patrons. The resource sharing networks and programmes of libraries facilitate activities like borrowing material not available in a specific library from other participating libraries. Such loans between libraries is known as an inter-library loan. It is a frequent responsibility of the circulation department.

The inter-library loan is perhaps the oldest form of cooperation among libraries. Inter- library loan operations can be divided into two: those relating to borrowing and those relating to lending. Both these activities are a more complicated variation of the general circulation functions.

When a reader makes a request for an item not in the library, efforts are made to identify other libraries which may be having that particular item in their collection. This procedure is simplified if proper tools like union lists and union catalogues are available. Once the libraries are identified, depending on the policy and procedure of inter-library loan arrangement a request is sent to a library owning the material through a standard form or letter. After the receipt of the requested book, the user is notified of its arrival and the item in charged out to him. In many libraries books acquired in a library on inter-library loan are not allowed to be taken out of the borrowing library to ensure its prompt return on requisition by the lending library, as also to safeguard against possible damage due to negligence. Once the user returned the book at the end of the loan period, it is in turn sent back to the owning library. The lending activities for the inter-library loan are initiated upon receipt of a requested letter from a borrowing library. Then the availability is checked using the library catalogue and other bibliographical tools. Once the item is located, it is sent to the requesting library. A record of these inter- library loan transactions are usually maintained separately in the form of a register.

9. Miscellancous Jobs

Other jobs which are involved in circulation section includes:

(i) Issues of reminders

(ii) Replacement of lost books

(iii) Replace of lost cards

(iv) Administration of property counter

(v) Provision of lockers etc.

Charging and Discharging Systems

The charging system which presently exists in Indian libraries, has evolved over a period of time. From a simple register system of recording loan transactions, circulation systems have now evolved into sophisticated computer-based systems.

There are some charging and discharging methods of documents which are in use. These can be broadly grouped as under.

1. Register systems
2. Card systems
3. Semi-mechanical systems
4. Automated systems

1. Register Systems

The earliest method of charging books for home use was a relatively simple one of writing the author, title and borrower's name in a 'Day book'. A 'Day book' was a register that recorded all daily transactions sequentially in a register. Later, this method was superseded by the 'Ledger system' with separate pages for each registered borrower. Each borrower's transactions where recorded, in his/her respective page. This avoided the tedium of searching through the 'Day book' for a single entry. The 'ledger systems' remained in use until the middle of the nineteenth century.

The disadvantage of both the 'Day book' and 'Ledger' systems was the absence of a mechanism to locate the whereabouts of the books. A solution to this shortcoming was found in the 'Dummy System'. In this system a block of wood or cardboard about the size of an ordinary book was covered with sheet of ruled paper on the back of which was entered the number of the borrower, call number, title of the book and date of issue. The wooden dummy was filed on the shelf in place of the book that was withdrawn. This method eliminated the need for going through lists of names and titles to find a specific book. This method made possible, for the first time, to identify of both the borrower and the book charged out.

The next step forward was the development of the 'Temporary Slip System'. In this system, a slip is prepared at the time of issue of a book, with the particulars of the book such as the call number, author title, and the particulars of the borrower, i.e., name registration number, address, etc., and the date of issue. These slips are arranged at the counter either datewise, or by alphabetically in the name of the borrowers or the registration numbers of borrowers. These slips are either destroyed or given back to the reader as receipt upon the return of the bocks. The main advantage of this system over the ' Dummy system' was that it kept the circulation record together at the circulation counter instead of scattering throughout the shelves. These temporary slips were later replaced by a permanent slip or a card for each book.

2. Card Systems

With the increase in the number of readers using libraries, it became necessary to devise some method of identifying both the book and the borrower. Thus the two card system, one card for the book and one for the borrower came into existence. First, identification cards were used, which were later substituted by borrower's card on which all book transactions were entered.

Of the two card systems, two systems, namely the Browne and the Newark are popular and widely used even today in libraries, particularly in India.

(A) Browne Charging System

The Browne Charging System was devised by Nina E. Browne who was librarian of the Library Bureau in Boston and served as the Secretary of the Publishing Board of the American Library Association.

Even though the system originated in the United States, it is not much in use in the country of its origin, but it has become quite popular in India.

(i) Equipment and material used: The special equipment and stationary material required to operate the system are the following:

(a) Registration cards of all borrowers arranged alphabetically.

(b) Borrower's tickets or pockets. Each borrower is given as many tickets/pockets of manila or rough paper as he/she is entitled. This ticket is in the shape of a pocket of 7.5×5.0 cms size with openings on two sides. This ticket bears the names and address of the borrower, the date of expiry of membership. In many libraries, a code number is devised and written/typed on the top of the card to represent category/subject of interest and date of validity of the membership. It also bears the signature and stamp of the librarian and the signature of the borrower on it.

(c) Book cards of size 10.25 × 5.0 cms bearing the call number; accession number, author and title of the book.

(d) Book pockets of size 12.5 × 7.5 cms which are pasted on the inside back/front cover of the book. The book cards are kept in these pockets when they are not in circulation.

(e) Date slip on which the date due or date of issue are stamped, to be pasted on the back or front flyleaf of the book.

(f) Date stamp and ink pad.

(g) Date guide cards.

(h) Charging trays.

(i) Circulation statistical sheets.

(j) Reminder cards, reservation cards, overdue fine slips, etc.

(ii) Charging Routine: Charging is the issue of books that are presented at the circulated counter to borrowers. This routine involves the following steps:

(a) The book to be borrowed and the borrower's ticket are presented by the user to the assistant at the circulation desk counter.

(b) The counter assistant after the identification of the reader either by familiarity through the identification card/ membership card, takes the book card out of the book pocket and slips it into the borrower's ticket/pocket.

(c) The due date is stamped on the due date slip pasted on the back or from the fly leaf of the book and the charged book is handed over to the patron.

(d) The book card coupled with the reader's pocket is filed in the charging tray behalf the respective due date card by call number.

(e) The call number and the borrower number are recorded in the daily circulation statistics sheet.

(iii) Discharging Routine : Discharging is the work of securing books borrowed and release the borrower's tickets. This routine work involves the following:

(a) When the book is presented at the counter for return, the due date/issue date is ascertained from the due date slip.

(b) The book card coupled with the reader's ticket is picked up from behind the appropriate date-guide card from the charging tray.

(c) The due date/issued date is cancelled on the due date slip and the reader's ticket is returned to the reader.

(d) The book card inserted into the book pocket and the book is thus discharged and the reader is absolved of his responsibility.

(e) It the book is returned after the due date, due overdue amount is computed and an overdue charged slip is given. The reader's ticket is returned only after the receipt for the overdue charge is presented.

(iv) Reserves: 'Reserves' constitute a facility of a circulation system by which a reader can reserve a book that is out on loan. This facility is built into a charging system. The routine involved is explained below:

If there is a request for reservation of a book in circulation, the reserve ticket is filled up by the reader and the reserve ticket containing the details of the book and the reader is inserted into the reader's pocket in the charging tray. When that book 'on hold' is returned the reserve card along with the book card will be slipped into the book pocket and the book will be kept in a special sequence and intimation will be sent to the reader who has reserved the book.

Advantages

1. Being simple procedure, results in economy of time and efforts are noticed.
2. Issue of reminders and calculation of fine.
3. Statistics of issue can be prepared easily.
4. Reserves and recalls can be carried out promptly.
5. No signatures are required at the time of issue/return.

Disadvantages

1. No permanent record of issue is available.
2. The reader has no record of the books borrowed by him.

3. Difficult to ascertain the number of books issued to a person as the borrowed tickets are scattered.
4. In case of loss of tickets, misuse of tickets is possible as signature of the reader is not necessary.
5. Caution and vigilance are necessary while inserting book, cards into the readers pocket as they are only one record of issue.

Call No.		Acc. No.
Name Of The Library		
The following books were issued/are due in the below mentioned dates		
Date of Issue/ Due date	Date of Issue/ Due date	Date of Issue/ Due date

Size : 12.5 cms × 7.5 cms

Date Slip

Brief Library Rules And Instruction

Size 12.5cms × 7.5 cms

Book Pocket

Call No.	Acc. No.
Author : ____________	
Title: ____________	

Size: 10.25 cms × 5.0 cms

Book Card

Name Address Date Of Expiry Signature of the Borrower

Size : 7.5 × 5.0 cms

Borrower's tickets

Specimens of Materials required in Browne System

B. Newark Charging System

This system was introduced in the Public library of Newark of New Jersey State in the USA in the year 1900.

(i) Equipment and Materials Used

It requires more equipment and materials than Browne Charging System. These are :

1. Registration file of all borrowers arranged in one alphabetical sequence and also have a numerical file of numbers assigned to each borrower.
2. Borrower's cards bearing the name, address and registration number of each registered borrower.
3. Book cards bearing call number author and title of book.
4. Date slip pasted on the front or back of book.
5. Book pockets giving the call number, author and title, date stamp and Ink pad.
6. Date guide cards for filing circulation cards.
7. Fine record slips and circulation statistical sheets.
8. Overdue reminder cards, reserved cards etc.

(ii) Charging routines : Charging routines are a little more elaborate and time consuming in this system than in the Browne Charging System. The steps involved in charging are follows:

(a) Borrower's Cards are presented by the user to the assistant at the circulation counter.

(b) The due date or date of issue, whichever is used, is stamped on the date slip in the book by the assistant.

(c) Similarly the due date is stamped on the book card taken out of the book-pocket and the borrower's card.

(d) The borrower's number is written opposite the date in the book-card and filed behind the concerned date-guide card.

(e) The borrower's card and the book are returned to the patron. Thus, the book is duly charged.

(iii) Discharging routines: The steps involved in discharging routines are:

(a) When the book is presented for return along with the membership card, date of return is stamped on the borrower's card, thus cancelling the charge for the book. The borrower's card is returned to the patron.

(b) The book card is located in the circulation file from the date on the date slip and placed in the book pocket.

(c) If the book is returned after the due date, the fine is computed and collected. The date of return is stamped only after the fine is paid.

(iv) Reserves: Reservation procedure is similar to the Browne Charging system. The reserve ticket filled in by reader is attached to the borrower's card in the charging tray/ when the particular book 'on hold' in returned, the reserve card along with the book card is pinned with the borrower's card and the book is kept in a special sequence and intimation is then sent to the reader who has reserved the book.

Advantages

(a) There is a permanent record of the number and type of books circulated and the kind of books borrowed by each reader.

(b) It is possible to know at all times, where a given book is, to whom it is charged, and when it is due.

(c) The record of the number of times a book has been circulated is available even when the book is not in the library.

(d) Since the transaction is recorded both on the borrowers' card as well as on the book cards the danger of dislocation is minimum.

If the borrowers' cards are lost, the record on the book cards is available and vice-versa.

(e) Several assistants can carry on the routines simultaneously.

(f) The borrowers can be allowed to borrow books from any branch library of a larger library system, provided there is a central registration file at the main library where an alphabetically arranged copy of all branch registrations is available.

Disadvantages

(1) Routines are slow, and cumbersome. The procedure of writing/stamping of the date of issue/due date and the borrower's membership number on the book cards and writing/stamping of issue/due date on the borrower's cards are time-consuming.

(2) There are chances of inaccuracies creeping in, especially when transcribing borrowers' card numbers. This is particularly true during rush hours.

(3) Two registration files are necessary: an alphabetical file by borrower's name and addresses and a file of registration numbers assigned to each borrower.

On the whole, the Newark System is considered to be foolproof and safe. This advantage may not always be available.

Call No: Acc No: Name of the Library This Book was issued/is due on the date last stamped or marked.

Size 12.5 × 7.5 cms.

Date Slip

Open Flap
Name of the Library Brief Library Rules 1. 2. 3. 4.

Size: 12.5 × 7.5 cms

Book Pocket

Name of the Library Call No: Acc. No: Author : Title: This Book was issued/is due on the date last stamped or marked.

Size: 10.0 × 5.0 cms

Book Card

<table>
<tr><td colspan="4">Name of the Library
Borrower's No: ____________________
Date of Expiry : ____________________

NON-TRANSFERABLE

The following books were issued to me.
Signature</td></tr>
<tr><td>Due date/
Date of Issue</td><td>Date of Return</td><td>Due date/
Date of Issue</td><td>Date of Return</td></tr>
<tr><td></td><td></td><td></td><td></td></tr>
<tr><td></td><td></td><td></td><td></td></tr>
</table>

(These columns are repeated on the reverse of the card)

Borrowers' Card

<table>
<tr><td colspan="4">Name of the Library
NON-TRANSFERABLE
Membership-cum-Identity Card</td></tr>
<tr><td colspan="4"></td></tr>
<tr><td>Due date/
Date of Issue</td><td>Date of Return</td><td>Due/date/
Date of Issue</td><td>Date of Issue</td></tr>
<tr><td></td><td></td><td></td><td></td></tr>
<tr><td></td><td></td><td></td><td></td></tr>
<tr><td></td><td></td><td></td><td></td></tr>
<tr><td></td><td></td><td></td><td></td></tr>
<tr><td></td><td></td><td></td><td></td></tr>
<tr><td></td><td></td><td></td><td></td></tr>
</table>

Membership-cum-identity Card

Specimen of the Materials required in Newark Charging System

(3) Semi-automatic Circulation System

The next stage saw the replacement of human labour by machines when mechanical charging systems were developed, essentially most subsequent systems, involved the use of cards with pre-punched holes around the edges, one of which could be cut to indicate the date on which an item is due. The cards are arranged by call number in a single sequence. The insertion of a knitting needle through a given hole will allow all the books overdue for a given date to fall free of the bunch of punched cards. This system is characterised by inventory and data access but placed a greater burden on the borrower. A borrower had to write the borrower's name and address and the call number, author and title of a book borrowed.

(4) Automated Circulation System

For several decades now, ingenious librarians and library equipment manufacturers in western countries have designed circulation systems using the latest technology. The advent of the computer in the 1960s and micro-computers in the 70s and 80s radically altered ground rules. Now all sequences of encoded elements are possible and information on any management data can be derived. Important statistical data pertaining to collection use and library users can be obtained by manipulating the data accumulated in the circulation process. However library automation extends beyond circulation functions into the more integrated systems of cataloguing, acquisitions, decision support systems and virtually all other library operations. Advantages of speed, the ability to manage large amounts of data, and the long term trends of increasing computer power and decreasing cost have attracted libraries to automated circulation.

In the developed countries of the world, it is now possible for all bout the smallest libraries to have access to and control their material through the current range of computers. The situation in India may not be as promising; however a slow process of change is taking place in at least the special libraries towards computerisation. The computers were expected to enter other types of libraries too in the coming years or so. An increasing number of university and college libraries already are to be moving towards automated circulation systems. The situation now seems to be quite encouraging.

2(D) Reference Section : Policy Work and Orientation Programme

Q. : Write an essay on Reference Section of library.

Or

Justify the need of Reference Section in libraries and describe its functions.

Ans. Reference section is one of the sections of the library, which is basically established to provide reference service to the readers. It is also known as the 'Heart of the Library' because a reader would not be able to find any thing from the library untill he is assisted by the staff of that particular section who are basically reference staff. Just starting from quick reference queries upto long range questions are solved by the reference - staff for the purpose, reference section houses such materials as bibliographies, encyclopedias, dictionaries, directories, as well as monographs, treatises and textbooks on a variety of subject.

The reference section within a library has two principal functions. It is firstly a collection of literature maintained wholly, or chiefly, for use on the library premises by people wishing to pursue specific study or research, secure in the knowledge that, as distinct from the home-reading library, the material that they require will always be available to them when required. Secondly, the reference department is designed as a collection to satisfy the needs of enquiries seeking specific factual items of information.

Need of Reference Section

The reference section in a library is needed because of following:

(i) Current Awareness Needs

People want to be uptodate. They want to read latest books, and know the latest news. It is particularly important for professionals in different fields to keep themselves abreast of latest developments in their profession. It is of regular nature and does not concentrate on a particular topic. It is rather general.

(ii) General Reading Needs

There may be very varied with some people, less varied with others, such as devotees of romantic or detective novels. Many people want to read for pleasure, while some others read in connection with hobbies and similar things, still other category of users need to read professional literature of current awareness nature.

(iii) Quick-reference Needs

There are everyday type of needs felt by persons while performing their normal duties. These needs are generally factual in nature like finding the correct spelling of a word, date of birth of a prominent personality, name of a person holding a particular position, etc. They are quite simple needs but often very urgent. Quick-reference needs are likely to be rather irregular, unlike current awareness needs, which will normally be constant.

(iv) Personal Problems

A person faces many crises in his life, and special needs arise because of them. It might be for information on a disease, or help in finding another job, or solving some administrative problem. They may be less frequent with majority of the persons.

(v) Personal Development

If a person begins a course of study on a new subject, or starts a higher level course in his area of interest, then he will need information including reading materials, to successfully complete the course. To some extent personal development needs may relate to less formal study too.

(vi) Research and Related Needs

These needs are generally felt by persons while planning a new research project. They require an exhaustive retrieval of existing literature or information on a topic. These needs are intended to know the existing state of affairs on a topic so that new study can be planned to take to existing knowledge one step ahead.

(vii) Artificiality of Cataloguing

The catalogues in the libraries are prepared according to certain codes, about which a new reader is not known. To make aware about the use of catalogues, reference service or the assistance of staff is needed.

(viii) Saving of Time

As trained staff of reference section satisfies the queries of readers within a reasonable time, reader's time is saved which he can utilize in other works.

(ix) Artificiality of Books

Today, with the advancement of printing technology, documents are coming in variety of forms. The knowledge is represented in the various forms as books, journals, audio/video and CDs etc. A new reader is not known about the use of many of these types of documents. In the libraries, staff of reference section assists him in getting desired information from the varied types of documents.

(x) Psychological Need

Above all, any reader who comes to a library, wants his desired study materials early. If within a reasonable time, his desires not completed there is always a possibility of decreasing his interest as the time passes. So, there should be atleast some one in the library, who could attend him and assist him in getting his desired study materials. This is only the reference section and its staff who can assists him and help in getting desired materials from the library.

So, a library can not work efficiently without a good reference section.

Functions of Reference Section

The functions of reference section in a library may be:

(i) Routine Work

The routine work involves the up-dating of loose-leaf reference services by the insertion of amendments as issued, checking receipts of periodicals and other subscription services and following up the non-receipt of parts with the suppliers, collecting material before ending to the binders, cataloguing new acquisitions, maintaining current information files and, of course, the acquisition of new stock. Such of this work is little more than simple drudgery, but it is essential to the creation of an efficient library, and it is important that all staff appreciate how crucial it is that such work is carried out properly, and how damaging slip-shod work can be to the reputation of the library in the eyes of its users-if a mis-filed periodical part urgently needed can not be found for example.

Many of the routine tasks of the reference library are monotonous and, if left in the hands of one member of staff for too long, will result in poor-quality work though sheet boredom and lack of concentration. Thus, the accurate shelving of books and clearing of requisition-slips from stack-shelves must be meticulously maintained, despite the uninteresting nature of the work; equally, the supervision of the returned books point in the reading-room must not be allowed to become perfunctory. In the interests of variety of work and full staff training, many of the routine tasks should be regularly rotated amongst staff members. Some tasks should be regularly rotated amongst staff a judicious mixture of work for each staff member, with every on having define responsibility for some function or functions, is essential. Staff members who know they have clear responsibility and are being relied upon are much more likely to be careful and orderly in their work than staff who feel they have no particular responsibility or importance in the whole scheme.

(ii) Enquiry Work

Even the 'public face' of enquiry work must be backed up by a definite routine to ensure that all enquiries received are dealt with on time and to the limit of the competence of the whole staff. Enquiries are received in a number of ways-by direct application to the staff in person, by telephone, or by letter or telex. Many of the direct person to-person enquiries can be dealt with on the spot as received, but for those more complex or time-consuming, and those received by letter, some kind of log or diary should be kept to ensure that all are dealt with properly. The most usual way of doing this is by entering details of all non-routine enquiries received in a desk-diary kept for that purpose, or on specially designed forms. It is necessary to make a regular review of all enquiries in progress at least once a day, with all new staff coming on duty being made aware of the nature of the work outstanding in case an enquirer returns to check progress on his enquiry. A staff conference on all enquiries in progress every morning is a good plan.

This need not take long and need not be formal, but all staff members will have some experience to contribute to the solution to difficult enquiries, a staff conference has the additional benefit developing the experience and skills of junior staff through the view of their seniors on the sources and methodology to be adopted.

(iii) Quick Reference Service

As indicated above, most enquiries received will be solved using the library's own resources. It is also the case that most enquiries are for specific, short answers, using a relatively small proportion of the total reference library stock-directories, dictionaries, bibliographies, encyclopedias and other reference compendia such as Whitaker's almanack, Statesman's yearbook, Keesings Contemporary Archives and The Guinness Book of Records, it is usual to group such quick reference' material close to the entrance to the library and adjacent to the main enquirey point. This gives the staff quick access to heavily-used material to answer urgent telephone enquiries, for example. It also encourages users to help themselves rather than wait for library staff to attend to them, but at the same time enables the staff to identify enquirers who are obviously floundering and need assistance. The provision of a quick reference collection reduces disturbance of long-stay users in the library through constant traffic to and from heavily used items shelved in the main sequence.

(iv) Guidance

Time to time, general guide-lines are also provided by reference section to its readers.

(v) Compilation of Study-Aid Materials

As stated earlier, there are available various types of documents in the library in which information and knowledge is dispersed. A reader does not have much time to find out and collect his relevant literature from this dispersed materials. If he spares much time in finding out relevant materials he will not be able to do his research work efficiently. So reference section compile the list of related books, abstract from journals and also prepares bibliography on the subjects asked for.

So we can see lot of work is done by the reference section of the library for satisfaction of its readers.

2(E)
Periodical Section

Q. : Explain the procedure for procurement of periodicals. How it is different from procurement of books?

or

Describe the functions of periodical sections in the library. Explain the use of three-card system in this context.

or

Describe 'Cardex' system used for controlling periodicals in the library.

or

How should you acquire the periodicals for a library? Justify the utility of 'Three Card System" of Dr. Ranganathan for maintaining their records.

Ans. : Periodicals are the primary source of information and awareness and are invariably more up-to-date than those of books. All the information on discoveries appear in periodicals in no time of their formulation. Whereas the same might take quite a considerable time before it can be included in the book form. It can be said that most of the material reported in periodicals is never published in books. That is the reason for keeping long files of back volumes of periodicals in the library.

A periodical is defined as "a publication issued in successive parts usually at regular intervals and as a rule intended to be continued indefinitely" by A.L.A. Glossary of Library Terms. On the other hand, Ranganathan defines a periodical publication as a Conventional Document of Kind-I with the following attributes:

(1) A volume, or a small group of volumes of it, is intended to be published or completed normally once in a year (or at other regular intervals), though irregularity in interval is not ruled out.

(2) Each successive volume, or periodical group of volumes, is usually distinguished by the year of publication and/or by a number belonging to system of simple or complex ordinal number. Such a number is usually called the *Volume Number.*

(3) The intention may be to continue the publication of the volumes for ever, though not actually be carried out.

(4) The intention may be to continue the same title in all the volumes, though this may not actually be carried out.

On the other hand, a serial is defined as "a publication in printed form or not issued in successive parts usually having numerical or chronological designations and intended to be continued indefinitely". Thus, the term serial encompasses an extremely wide range of material including journals/periodicals, newsletters, newspapers, technical and research reports, yearbooks and annuals, and national and international government publications.

A big library, maintaining a periodical section is involved in varied operations causing series of problems. These operations vis-à-vis problems such as ordering, making advance payment for subscription, receipt of periodical etc. look simple but are extremely complex in practice.

Generally, periodical in a library are acquired by following means.

(a) Acquisition Through Gifts

Gifts constitute an important source for the acquisition of periodicals in the library. For example, many societies send their periodicals/ publications to the library free of cost for the sake of publicity. Some publications also supply some of their periodicals for some time to make the libraries subscribe to them at a later data. However, the indiscriminate acceptance of gifts may create administrative problems pertaining to storage, processing, maintenance, cost, etc. Hence they should be accepted with much care and scruting after ascertaining their usefulness to the users of the library concerned.

(b) Acquisition Through Exchange

Acquisition of periodicals through exchanges is another mechanism by which Collection Development can takes place. The two commonest forms of exchange are on a piece-for-piece basis or on a value-for-value basis. In the former method a publication has to be sent in exchange for another publication irrespective of its cost, where as in the latter case, the exchange is based on the costs of the publications covered by the exchange relationship. The former has the advantage of not requiring much accounting provided that a reasonable and suitable item is sent or received in exchange. If the value of the item received is uncertain it may be advisable to insist on a closer degree of equality in respect of the materials sent.

Smithsonian Institution, USA, offers for example the exchange of their publications with those interested organisations of various countries. Similarly, there is an exchange mechanism between DRTC and IASLIC for exchange of serials/publications. Perhaps, exchange agreements between institutions concerned is a necessary prerequisite for a successful exchange programme.

(c) Institutional Membership

Institutional membership is another potential resource of building up a periodical/serial collection. Learned societies generally publish one or more regular publications to communicate their activities, programmes and achievements to their members regularly. Hence, the library will do well to enlist itself as a member of learned societies and thus will be able to receive the periodical publications either free of cost or at confessional prices.

(d) Acquisition Through Purchase

Two different methods are available for ordering of periodicals. They are the *direct subscription method* and the *agency method.* In the former case, the library places orders directly with the publishers of each periodical. In the latter case, the order is placed with an agent who acts as the intermediary between the library and the publishers.

When we acquire periodicals through subscription, it needs some steps to be followed. These are discussed below.

1. Job before ordering

Being the requirement of authorities, libraries have to invite quotations for appointing vendor. This leaves no choice and the vendor though not reliable is tolerated only because of his lowest quotations. The other major hurdle is uncertain budget. The funds are always deficit and that too are not sure of their release. The prices of periodicals are constantly rising without raising the budget. Irregularity in sending subscription is also a problem, which means irregular supply of issues of periodical and cutting of budget means reducing the subscribed journals. Sometimes there may be defective and wrong supply. Reminders are issued to give attention to this effect. The returning of unrelated supply is also a problem.

2. Preliminaries

In the selection of periodical publication, the priority should be to receive the most required journals only. As far as possible money should be shared (i) by exploring the possibility of getting certain periodicals on exchange basis; (ii) by becoming members of societies of getting their publication in cheaper rates; (iii) by receiving journals on gifts; (iv) the receiving the periodical of lesser use on inter Library loan; and by resource sharing.

3. Vendors

In small libraries, generally one Indian Vendor for both Indian and Foreign periodical publications is preferred. But, for big libraries, there may be several categories of vendors such as:

(i) Indian Vendor for Indian Journals.

(ii) (a) Foreign vendor for foreign journals.

(b) For Indian sole agent representing foreign publisher of a journal.

(iii) Subscribing directly from the concerned publisher (s).

(iv) Through quotation select vendors appointed by foreign publishers and further vendors may be allowed renewal of subscription by the libraries on the basis of satisfactory performances of supply in the previous year.

(v) *Terms and Conditions* : Good Office's Committee (GOC) is a voluntary organization formed to stabilize and introduce uniform terms and supply to libraries, to ensure a fair working margin to book sellers and an efficient service to libraries. Committee has laid down terms and conditions for supply of journals to the subscribers in India.

4. Ordering Procedure

As has been said earlier, current periodicals are acquired by various methods , i.e., (i) subscription orders, (ii) membership of professional societies, (iii) exchange, (iv) gifts. The greater number of periodicals are acquired through subscription order. Exchange method is very useful in the cities where there are several big libraries.

At the time of making order, complete bibliographical details like name of the title, publisher/distributor, volume number and year are mentioned. Bills are requested in triplicate. The journals are received by air mail or surface mail as suited to a library. In case of the periodicals which are continuously preserved, the policy of standing order is good and convenient.

Quotations are also invited for the supply of back journals. The vendor appointed through quotation may be appraised of the terms regarding the publications to be supplied. But care should be taken that if other neighbouring libraries have already preserved the same journals, then microfilm copies may be preferred.

5. Payment

According to normal procedure, a library has to make advance payment to the vendor. But it depends on the mutual agreement whether to make full advance payment or some part of payment is detained. Many libraries follow GOC rates of exchange, but others pay according to Bank Exchange rates.

Precaution : Payment of subscription of periodical publication is done periodically, weekly fortnightly or monthly as the case may be. The bill is checked with the register card and the current amount claimed is verified. Then voucher number and date are entered in the register card to avoid duplicate payment.

Refund of amount is allowed in case the publication is ceased. The amount may be refunded or adjusted if it is incomplete supply. Case of missing issues are also amicably settled.

6. Procedures of recording the receipt of Periodicals

There are a number of methods of recording the receipt of periodicals in a library such as-

Register System

Ledger System

Card System

Three Card System

Kardex

(i) Register System : In small libraries receiving up to two or three dozens periodicals, the Register system may be used allotting one or two pages each for mothlies, quarterlies, half yearlies, yearlies etc. The page contains the following informaticn.

Year ....

Sr. No.	Title	Vol. & year	Publi-sher	Ven-dor	Period Jan....Dec.	Ann. Sub.	Vr. No. & date	Re-marks

The page for dailies and weeklies may contains following information:

Sr. No.	Title	Vol. year & month	Publi-sher	Ven-dor	Period 1,2,...31	Sub.	Vr. No. & date	Re-marks

(ii) Ledger System : In this system, the record is kept in the form of a bound register wherein each page is allotted to a periodical. On top of the page usually, details like the name of the periodical, its periodicity, the name of the publisher/sponsor, the name of the supplier, the amount and period of subscription paid, etc., are written. Columns are provided for year and months, volume and number, date of receipt and remarks. Entries will be made in these columns as and when current issues are received. A sample page of this register is given below. The major advantage of this system is that each page will explain the receipt of the various issues of a periodical.

This method may be found satisfactory for a small library subscribing to a few periodicals. This chief disadvantages of the system are that each page has to be examined in order to take note of the non-receipt or overdue issues at a point of time.

	Payment		
	Vol. or Year	Ann. Sub.	Voucher no. & date
Title Pulisher Vendor Class number Periodicity Order number and date			

Year & Vol.	Jan	Feb	Mar	Apr.	May	June	July	Aug	Sep	Oct	Nov	Dec	Remarks

(iii) Card System : The Card System can overcome many of the disadvantages of the Ledger System. In this system, cards of a uniform size, either 5" × 3" or 6" × 4", can be used where each card can hold the data relating to a particular periodical. The card can contain all the details normally found in the Ledger System. If separate cards are to be used for the different volumes of a periodical, the card can contain additional information like the reminders sent, claims made, etc.

(iv) The Three Card System : Three Card System is a method introduced by Ranganathan. In this system, three different cards of the size 5" × 3" are maintained for each periodical. They are called the Register Card, the Check Card, and the Classified Index Card.

Register Card : The Register Card records the information like Title of Publication, Vendor, Class number, Periodicity, Order Number and date, note: volume or year, Annual subscription, voucher number, date of payment, Volume & issue No., date of publication & date of receipt etc. Once the bill has been passed, the entry are made in the Register of payments and serial number allotted to the entry in this register which is called voucher number. The register cards are arranged alphabetically by title of journal. The register system is useful for:

(i) Complete data of issue including its receipt and non-receipt.

(ii) Knowing about payment made or not and how much.

(iii) When the particular issue received and how much delayed.

(iv) Whether or not a particular journal is being subscribed to.

Title			PAYMENT		
Publisher			Vol or year	Ann. Sub.	Voucher No. and date
Vendor					
Class number			Periodicity number and date	Order	
Note					
Vol. and No.	Date of Pub.	Date of rect.	Vol. and No.	Date of Pub.	Date of rect.

Register Card

Note: The columns for vol. and no. date of publication and date of receipt are repeated at the back of the register card.

Check Card: Check Card contains information as under:

Title, Periodicity, Vol. & Issue No., Date of reminder, Initials of Librarian This system keeps a watch about the receipt of different issues and reminders the person handling the system as and when the issue becomes over due. Hence, it is useful for sending reminders.

Check Card are divided into 52 groups on the basis of the week during which the next issue is due.

Vol. and No.	Rem Date	L's Init-ials	Vol and No.	Rem. Date No.	L's Init-ials	Vol. and No.	Rem. Date	L's Init-ials	Vol. and No.	Rem. Date	L's Init-ials

Check Card

Note: The columns giving vol and no, Rem date and L's initials are repeated at the back of the check card.

Classified Index Card: This card shows the volumes available in the library in the case of each periodical. It also gives details about the supplements, cumulative indexes, etc of the periodical. These cards, as their names imply, are arranged in a classified order according to the Class Numbers given to periodicals.

Cl. No.	Ann. Subs.	Per.
Title		
Vendor		
Publisher		
Vols. available		
Indexes, etc.		
Supplements, etc.		

Classified Index Card

Being arranged in classified order, one can know which periodical publications are being received by the library in a given subject. With this system available index in a particular subject can be prepared.

Routine of Three Card System: To start with, when the mail is received, each packet is opened after checking its right address. The unpacked issues are arranged alphabetically. After examining these to be the sound copies, entries are made in the register card at the right place. Next step is to put down class number taken from the covers, plates first and last bages. Space is left for the gap issues which are expected to be received later on. Reminder are sent to the vendor for the supply of issues not received in time after allowing some grace period. If the issue is a gift, then acknowledgment is also sent.

Once registration of an issue is over, the same is tallied in the check card. The check card makes the official vigilant about the non-receipt issues.

Three card system is simple, efficient and economical in time and money.

(v) **Kardex System :** This system was introduced by the Remington Rand of India, Ltd. It is a type of visible record system maintained in a steel filing cabinet. Each unit cabinet contains seven trays in all providing more than 500 card holders. Each card holder can hold two cards, a Bottom Card and a Top Card. The top card is fitted opposite to the bottom card. It lies verso of the next card holder such that when any card holder for a given title is lifted, then both cards-bottom and the top, face each other.

The top card is meant for the payment made to the vendor. One card with sides, has the capacity of covering the entries of 20 Volumes.

The bottom card is useful for providing information such as:

(a) Total periodical holdings of the library.

(b) Latest issues received in the library.

(c) Information regarding gaps.

(d) To guide the location of a particular volume.

(e) Useful for indicating overdue issue for which reminder might be sent.

(f) The records of reminders may also be maintained in these bottom cards.

Name of the Library__________________________________

Frequency : W/F/M/Q/HY/A

Year	No / Vol	1	2	3	4	5	6	7	8	9	10	11	12	T.P.	Reminder

Volumes per Year

Nature of Binding   In Bindery   Library has   Location

Title   Jan. Feb. Mar. Apr. May June July Aug ... Dec.

....

Type along the dotted line, then fold pack or detach the stub

Specimen of the Bottom Card

In this system, the card is fixed in the punched holes of the card holder and plastic tag is put at the mouth, when next issue is due, Tag fall down or get misplaced quite often therefor in actual practice, many libraries have abandons the use of plastic tags.

Volume Number	Date of Publication	Date of Reciept of Bill	Voucher Number	Amount of Subscription	Agent	Volume Number	Date of Publication	Date of Recipt of Bill	Voucher Number	Amount of Subscription	Agent

Specimen of the Top Card

7. Display of the Periodicals

All the issues of the journals are displayed soon after its registration, on the periodical display racks so the proceeding issues be replaced with the new ones. The former issue may be kept in the boxes of the display racks or may be sent to the department concerned for readily available.

8. Accessioning of Complete volumes

When all the issues, its title page and index of a journal are received, it is collected (i.e. checking the issues with contents in proper sequence). The journal is now in a complete volume. The completed volume then may be accessioned in an accession register after binding.

9. Binding

The accessioned journals are sent for binding. Generally the journal have a half-leather binding. The bulky volumes are bound in parts, one volume may have two three or more parts as the case may be. The bound journal bears name of the title in brief, year, Vol. No. and the part (if any).

After the journals are received from binding these are processed i.e. classified and catalogued like books. Then the procedures of label pasting and writing and stamping are done to the journals. The journals complete and ready in all respects are sent for shelving or these may be sent to the departments concerned.

2(F)
Maintenance Section : Guiding, Shelving and Stock Rectification, Verification and Binding

Q. : Write an essay on Maintenance Section of a library.

Ans. The maintenance work of library documents in the library is an important as the other works of the library. In fact, the ultimate success of various other functions like acquisition, classification and cataloguing rests on the efficiency of maintenance work. No matter how well a collection is classified or catalogued, books cannot be serviceable to users unless proper care is taken to organise and maintain the book collection. Maintenance work involves continuous monitoring or the proper stocking, arrangement and display of books on the shelves in the stack rooms and taking care of them. This essentially implies two aspects:

(i) Organisation of the stack room and arrangements of books on the shelves

(ii) Conservation of books i.e., overseeing and supervising the physical conditions of books, overall cleanliness of the stack areas, etc.

In an open access library which allows users to browse, choose and select books of their interest, shelf organisation and arrangement of books are of primary importance. Books on different subjects that are constantly on demand are to be easily accessible to readers. This means that the professional classification schedules are rarely in tune with the layman's expectations of sequence of books on shelves. In a public library books of fiction, travelogues, biography may be more popular from the readers point of view than the more serious books on literature, sciences and social sciences. A classification scheme does not provide the sequence of subjects of books on their its popularity.

Besides, reference books like encyclopaedias, dictionaries, year books, directories, etc. should be kept in a separate place for easy reach and uninterrupted use by readers. Recent arrivals and books on current interest must be displayed at a prominent place to attract the attention of readers. Other books must be stacked according to their popular use with reference to the subjects.

Conventionally, in libraries, books are kept on open shelves which are usually arranged in parallel rows with passages from 75 to 80 cm in width between the rows. The normal height of the shelves is 190 to 205 cm which permits taking books from the upper most shelf. Single faced shelves are placed along the walls. Within the rooms themselves, between the aisles, the shelves are double-faced. Single faced sections have six or seven one metre shelves. While double faced sections have twelve to fourteen one metre shelves. Under these circumstances, taking into account all aisles and gangways and approaches only about 30 percent of the floor space is actually used for shelves themselves. The conventional shelving system is high on accessibility, but quite low on economy. For collections which are in active use or those that are open to free use by readers, the conventional shelving is considered to be more suitable. Compact shelves are a special type of storage equipment which makes possible a substantial increase in the capacity of storage space through various arrangements of units, sections and complete shelving systems, as well as adaptation of the shelf loading surface themselves. All revolving compact shelves use a suspended construction with vertically hung hinged sections of various types usually combined with a guide rail arrangement. It could be either double faced or single faced.

Compact shelving falls into the following types:

(i) Stationary shelves combined with movable revolving segments.

(ii) Stationary shelves with movable drawers, and

(iii) Movable sliding shelves.

As far as, current issues of Periodicals and Non-Book Material-Storing, Shelving and Arrangement is concerned, most libraries have periodical collections, the current issues having to be display for browsing/reading. Back numbers of them for a year stored along with current issues. Special display racks are available for this kind of storage and display.

Special storage facilities are also required for storing audio-visual materials, microfilms of newspapers, CD-ROMs, etc. which are acquired by university, research and other types of large libraries.

Here, the problems are their preservation and storing for ease of retrieval. They cannot be browsed and hence their shelving and storage need special attention.

Depending on the size of these collections, storage and arrangements aspects of these materials have to be considered. Special storage shelves are available which have to be thoughtfully acquired, satisfying all functional and service aspects.

The second aspect of maintenance work is book conservation. Only books in good physical condition should be allowed to stay on shelves. Constant shelf checking would remove torn, soiled and damaged books from shelves for repair, rebinding or to be withdrawn from circulation. This is a healthy practice and should never be under-estimated.

Another important aspect of conservation is that the stacks must be cleaned regularly to protect books from dust, dirt and insects. Air-conditioning of stack rooms would be ideal to protect books from dust, heat and moisture.

All these efforts are to aid the fundamental task of locating a book when it is wanted and returning to its assigned place when it is no longer needed; maintaining the order of books and taking care of the books that they are wanted again. All these tasks are usually entrusted to a maintenance section/division in addition to the other functions.

Broadly speaking, besides stacking, maintenance work include the following works to be done on regular basis.

(i) Dusting and Cleaning of Shelves : These are important and indispensable routines of libraries which have to be attended meticulously. Books have to be protected from dust and dirt. No room should be given to readers to complain about dust and dirt on the shelves. In a library where stack area is very large, cleaning can be done by mechanical devices like vacuum cleaners etc.

(ii) Shelving of New Books and Returned Books: The books received from the processing sections of the library need to be displayed for a week or ten days on the latest additions shelf, before are taken to the stacks for shelving. This may be a weekly activity. But books received from borrowers must be returned to the shelves regularly, preferably the same day so that they are readily available for use by others.

(iii) Shelf Study and Shelf Rectification: The maintenance staff at all levels in a library would do well to devote their free time to studying the books on the shelves so as to develop a fair knowledge of their contents. This knowledge is of vital importance to the efficiency of their work, particularly, in their relation to the reference section. An intimate knowledge of the book collection would be invaluable in answering reference enquiries which involves prolonged search.

Books are very often misplaced on the shelves by readers who browse through them. Readers are to be strictly instructed not to replace books on shelves but still it may happen quite often. A book wrongly placed is as good as lost. Hence restoring order among the books is absolutely essential. This work is referred to as shelf rectification.

(iv) Identifying Damaged/Torn Books for Reparing : Shelf study and shelf rectification would also enable the maintenance staff to identify books that need mending, repair, rebinding, etc. Unsoical elements could also multilate books which can be discovered during shelf study or rectification. These books have to be withdrawn from circulation temporarily till they are repaired or replaced by a fresh copy, if they are important.

(v) Shitting and Reshifting Books : In order to take away the monotony of appearance of shelf arrangement and to introduce an element of novelty, book have to be reshuffled to keep in tune with the changing popularity of subjects with the reading public. While this cannot be done too frequently, the entire library may be reshuffled once in five years. But this is necessary, though it involves extra work and some dislocation is service.

(vi) Assistance to Readers: Readers often need advice and help in locating and identifying books of their interest. Although reference assistant may do this job, the maintenance staff who have a closer knowledge of the contents of the library could go to the rescue of their colleagues in the reference section.

(vii) Maintenance of Book Tags: Book tags carry call number of books fixed at the bottom of books or on their spines. This helps the arrangement of books on the shelf. These book tags get damaged or worn out after repeated use and they have to be refixed if they get soiled. In many libraries, book tags have been replaced by tooling, a process by which call numbers of books could be written on the spines or at the bottom of the covers.

(viii) Maintenance of Shelf-List: Shelf list is an important record of books, which shows the position of any book on the shelves. In order to control the movements of books in a library, a shelf list is made which is maintained in standard size cards.

It enables the library to maintain correct sequence on the shelves. It can also indicate immediately the position of any book on the shelf. Shelf list is an important record, it should be kept under the safe custody and also kept up-do-date.

(ix) Stock Verification: Stock verification means physical check up of documents, which are on change or record of an information system. This is common practice in all organization whether it is a private or government department.

Strictly speaking it is undertaken to ascertain that all the books acquired by library can be accounted for. In a narrow sense, it means physical check up of documents but in a broader sense, it would means to have an assessment of the collection of documents.

Q. : Write an essay on Preservation of Books/ Reading materials in a library.

Ans. The preservation of books and other reading materials is an important aspect but a tough task for librarians. We know that a considerable proportionate of library budgets are apportioned for the purchase of books and journals in the library. It is imperative that due attention should be given so that it should not be damaged by its enemies. The money spent on its are not vital things but its values are the point of consideration. The role of the librarian therefore becomes significant. He is entrusted with the preservation of the books and publicizing them. A book may get damaged or defaced due to certain causes such as:

1. Climatic Factor such as :

   Light, Dust and Dirt

2. Various type of insects

3. Human being i.e., readers.

1. Climate Factors: Sudden variations in temperature and moisture, are two important factors responsible for the deterioration of the reading materials. They should be kept in a comparatively uniform temperature and in dry place. Various scientific methods can be employed for this purpose.

Direct sunlight also reduce the softness of paper and binding. Therefore efforts should be made to avoid direct sunlight.

Moisture, humidity, dampness, etc. are the different factors, which damage the books and journals. The moisture in air can be removed by proper ventilation in the stock room. Dampness ruins the paper and also becomes a breeding ground of many injurious insects.

Dust and dirt are also harmful to books. To avoid these dusting should be done in a warm and dry weather.

2. Insects : Several kinds of insects earth into wooden articles. These insects thrive in dampness and dust. Some of the insects are – Cockroach or Black Beetles; Termites or White ants; Silver fish; Book lice, Book worms; Fish insects; and Fungus too may prove destructive to the books.

(i) Cockroach or Black Beetles : These are normally found in warm countries. They eat away the binding and other gummed parts of the book. To kill these insects Gemmaxene or D.D.T. powder may be used. Alternatively these insects can be repelled by camphor and nepthalene. Fumigation and napthalene bricks are more effective to kill bookworms.

(ii) Termites or White Ants : These are the most injurious enemies of books. They eat wood, books, files and other valuable picture and catalogue cards of the library. Once these termites start destroying the books, it becomes very difficult to stop the process, as they based very fast. There are two categories of termites.

— Earth dwelling termites; and

— Wood dwelling termites.

To eliminate these termites chemically, carbon bisulphide or carbon tetrachloride are used. Solignum oil may also be used in stack rooms as a precaution.

(iii) Silver Fish : These also destroy the binding paper and starch at night. They perforate papers, prints, photographs, catalogue cards and card-board boxes. These insect can be removed, if a mixture of simple boric acid and flour is spreaded near the books. A mixture of sodium flouride and flour (12 : 100) would also be effective to remove them.

(iv) Book Lice : Book lice are very small sized insects and may be present in thousands of numbers between two pages of a musty book. Book lices can be avoided by using ethylene, carbondioxide and Formaldehyde vapours.

(v) Book Worms : Book worm is a generic term that includes the larvae of different beetles. These are mainly found in tropical and semi-tropical parts of world. They lay their eggs on the edges of books, generally on the bottom edges and shelves. Books damaged by beetles should be removed from the shelves immediately.

(vi) Fish Insects : These damage the books by eating the coloured parts of binding and damaging maps and other illustrations. To remove these, ethylene, carbon-dioxide and formaldehyde vapours are used.

(vii) Fungus : Though not in the category of insects, fungus is also injurious to books, which grows in humidity. It forms a thin whitish coating consisting of fungi of many kinds. Fungus destroys the paper and leather leaving white scars on the book. It can be removed by proper ventilation system. A loose shelving of books should be done to avoid the fungus. Hot air circulation may also be used to heat the shelves. A mixture of thymal crystal (100 grams), mercuric bichloride (4 grams), ether (200 c.c.) and benzene (400 c.c.) can also be used to destroy the fungus layers.

Important chemicals used to kill the insects

Insect	*Chemical used*
1. Cockroaches or black beetles	Thymol hydrocyanic gas, D.D.T., flit, tick-20 and belgoan carbon disulphide
2. Termites or white ants	Solignum oil
3. Silver fish	Dry heat. A mixture of Sodium flouride and flour (12:100)
4. Book lice	Ethylene and carbondioxide
5. Book worms	Napthalene bricks, solignum oil.

6. Fish insect	Ethylene and carbondioxide, formaldehyde vapours.
7. Fungus	Fynoil, hot air circulation, A mixture of thymal crystals (100 gm), Mercuric bichloride (4 gm), Ether (200 c.c.) and benzene (400 c.c.).

3. Human Beings or Readers : Some readers are in habit of stealing and mutilating the reading materials. Thus, they damage the library reading matter by:

(i) Misplacement : Some readers are in habit of placing the books at places other than the shelves they are supposed to be, thus other readers find it difficult to find the desired books at the right time and place.

(ii) Mutilation : A book made unfit for reading either wholly or partially by dog earing the pages, plates and pictures is termed as mutilation of the book. The act of mutilation of books by the readers is traceable broadly to :

(a) Shortage of time at the disposal of reader

(b) Idleness and sluggishness

(c) Vengeance and

(d) Mental ill health of reader.

(iii) Theft : Theft of reading material from library is a major problem throughout the world. A theft may be defined as carrying away of the reading material without prior permission of the librarian. In order to prevent the theft, manually controlled entrance and exit gate, strict vigilance in the stacks, reading rooms and other important places in the library and a through checking and search in at the exit are essential.

Generally it is observed that the readers who are not capable of copying the graphs and art plates etc. are tempted to take away them even against their conscience. Therefore, if there is a provision of reprographic service, this wrongful act may be avoided. Some more precautions are also suggested such as:

1. To be alert and check all visitors coming to library.
2. To keep an eye on doubtful readers.

3. No personal belongings should be allowed inside the library.
4. Pocket sized and other such smaller books should be kept under lock and keys.
5. The windows and doors of the library should be made theft proof as well as rat proof i.e., a netwire of steel meshes should protect books from being thrown out of the library.
6. Only one door should be kept open for exit and another of for entrance.

Besides, now-a-days, libraries have started to maintain a good collection of non-book materials. These also need proper conservation for the purpose, Their's handling includes proper care as they can be get destroyed easily. They should be handled carefully by the staff as well as by the readers. They also should be stored in appropriate places with moderate temperatures and humidity.

Q. : Distinguish between Stock Rectification and Verification or Taking. Describe the procedure for Stock Rectification without dislocating the services.

Ans. In library, books are very often misplaced on the shelf by readers who browse through them. Though the readers are strictly instructed not to replace books back on shelves yet still it may happen quite often. A book wrongly placed is as good as lost. Hence, restoring order among the books is absolutely essential.

The process of placing back the mis-placed books on their right places on the shelves by the staff in known as shelf rectification. Where as, the stock verification implies the physical check-up of the articles on record. The concept of Stock Verification is as old as the very concept of preparation of inventories of objects having a physical entity, namely stores of different kinds and descriptions.

In the present day context the Stock Verification may be defined as "An yearly compulsory mechanical exercise of orpetitive nature required by auditors causing inconvenience to library users by the libraries closure as well as acting as drudgery for the unwilling library staff and finally yielding unreliable results without any monetary gain leading to unnecessary harrassments and punishments to mostly innocent library staff."

Since books also have a physical entity, these are treated as stores for that purpose and since all stores are subject to audit control, so are the books and consequently libraries. Annual Stock Verification has therefore been an audit requirement in all libraries and the purpose is to find out the loss, if any and to fix the responsibility for the loss. Thus the whole idea of Stock Verification in libraries emanates from the concept of treating libraries as mere stores of books. However, with the development in the paper industry, its production of books at cheaper rates, the changes in the concept of functions and use of libraries as well as the services offered to clientele have made the task of Stock Verification very difficult and cumbersome, rather making it impossible to meet the audit requirements of losses found in stock taking on any one as losses depend largely on the moral tone of users rather than the library staff. Moreover the losses are not worth the amount of labour and headache involved in doing Stock Verification. Todays, most of the documents in the libraries are kept open to make their maximum use. Hence in open access system the books are allowed to be handled freely and it is natural that some percentage of the loaned books are bound to be lost.

Need of Stock - Taking

If some books are lost, it is essential to replace them so that no gap is created in the usual library services. This would be possible only if periodical physical check up of the library stock is made. But, on the other hand, it is suggested that those books which are important and popular and which must be replaced, can easily be found out since such books will be demanded constantly and if not found on the shelves and are not issued out can be deemed to be lost and can be replaced and so no special purpose may be served by regular stock - taking. Though, theoretically it may not be very essential to resort to regular stock-taking in view of the above mentioned suggestion, yet, in practice, it is both essential and desirable to have some kind of checking so that inherent defects in the administrative policies may be detected and possible remedies may be devised to eradicate these maladies.

The desirability or otherwise of stock - taking also depends upon the size of the book stock of a library. In big libraries, it becomes difficult, if not physically impossible, to do thorough checking at regular intervals and it also dislocates the regular rhythm of the library routines since some staff members working in essential services sections of the library are engaged in stock verification. There are libraries which close the library during stock- taking period or curtail some service. This practice runs counter to the basic principles of library service. In a library having less than 20,000 volumes, annual stock - checking is recommended and in the libraries with more than 20,000 volumes, sample - verification in every 3 years should be commenced.

Stock - Taking Methods

The prevalent methods of Stock - Taking are given below:

1. Stock - Taking by Accession Register.
2. Stock - taking by using a separate register with Accession Numbers.
3. Stock - Taking by preparing separate sheets which contain Accession Numbers in a consecutive order.
4. Stock - Taking by Numerical Counting.
5. Stock - Taking by the Shelf List having special columns on the cards for stock taking record.
6. Stock - Taking by Shelf List without any specific columns on the cards.
7. Combining of stock rectification and stock - taking processes.
8. Stock Verification with the help of computer.
9. Sample Stock Verification.
10. Stock - Taking by Duplicate Set of Book cards.
11. Stock - Taking by Master Record.

Important methods are being discussed here :

1. By Accession Register

This method is very simple. The Accession Register is taken to the shelves and one person calls the particulars of the books from the shelf alongwith the Accession Number and the other person ticks the concerned Accession Number in the Accession Register. When all the books are checked, a list of untraceable items is prepared and efforts are made to trace out the missing books.

This system though looks very simple, is very cumbersome and time consuming and it spoils the Accession Register. It is cumbersome because each time the particulars of a book are called by the person on the shelf, the other person which with the register has to find out the exact Accession Number by lifting many pages at a time. As such, there is a danger of mistakes. It is time - consuming because it takes a lot of times in finding out the exact Assession Number from the Accession Register since the books on the shelves are not arranged according to the Accession Numbers but are arranged according to the Call Numbers which represent the subject of the books. It spoils the Accession Register because when some mark either by pencil or pen is a made, it leaves behind some impression even though these marks are erased. Thus, the whole of the Accession Register is spoiled and a day comes when the Accession Register becomes unintelligible.

2. Stock - Taking by using Separate Register with Accession Numbers

If the Accession Register is used for stock - taking it is likely that it may be disfigured and even the life of the Register may be shortened because by constant handling, the paper will give way and an essential record may be lost. To prepare duplicate Accession Register, especially when the number of accessioned books runs into thousands and lakhs, is a stupenduous task. An alternative method is suggested by which a separate stock - taking register is prepared with the following columns :

Acc. No.	1996	1997	1998	19991	2000	2001	Remarks
25726							
25727							
25728							
25729							
25730							

In this method, the Stock - Taking Register is taken to the shelves. One person speaks out the Accession Number from the book and the other one ticks the relevant year column from the register against the spoken Accession Number. At the end of stock taking, a list is prepared on separate sheets, tracing of the untraceable books is done and the items found afterwards either from the Issue Record or binding Section or from the shelves are crossed from this list. The remaining items are noted down on a separate paper for getting them written off. All the relevant information about the books is given on this sheet and the price of these books totalled so as to find out the actual loss. The crossed items are tick marked in the Stock - Taking Register. In this way, stock-taking is completed.

This method, no doubt, is better than the previous one since it saves the Assession Register from wear and tear. The danger of speaking out wrong Accession Number or crossing out wrong number always remains there. This method also is very slow and it takes much time in stock verification. Hence, this method is not suitable for big libraries. Moreover, the Stock - Taking Register will be used for a limited number of years and again a new register will have to be prepared afresh every time the year columns are ticked. This is an unnecessary wastage of money, time and energy.

3. Stock - Taking By Preparing Separate Sheets Containing Accession Numbers

In order to obviate the necessity of getting printed the new Stock-Taking Register after some years or of preparing fresh Accession Register, a new and simple method can be used for stock verification by preparing separate sheets which have Accession Numbers upto the last item acquired in the library in a consecutive order as under:

Specimen Stock - Taking Sheets for 2003 - 2004

1.	~~11~~	21.	31.
2.	12.	22.	32.
3.	13.	23.	33.
4.	14.	~~24~~.	34.
5.	15.	25.	35.
6.	16.	26.	36.
7.	17.	27.	37.
8.	18.	28.	38.
9.	19.	~~29~~.	39.
10.	20.	30.	40.

This means that the books with Accession Numbers 11, 24 and 29 have been traced out. Similarly, all the traced items are to be crossed out and the remaining items are checked with the Charged Tray, Binding Tray and other sequences in the library such as Withdrawl Register etc. and the items found in these sequences are crossed on these sheets. The rest of the Accession Numbers are transferred on to separate sheets and detailed bibliographical information is noted against these Accession Numbers. These sheets are either got typed or the numbering is done by a numbering machine. In this method, the sheets can be multiplied and many persons at one time can do the stock - taking work. Thus, the whole of the work can be finished within a short time.

4. Stock - Taking By Numerical Counting

Another simple method of stock - taking found in foreign libraries is the mere counting of books on the shelves, charged trays and other sequences and the total thus arrived at is deducted from the total number of books accessioned according to the Accession Register. The balance indicates the number of books not traceable. This method gives a rough idea of the amount of loss and is adopted by those libraries which do not give undue importance to physical checking of each and every item in the library. This system does not serve the basic purpose for which stock - taking practice has been stated.

5. Stock - Taking By Register or Shelf List with Special Columns

All the above mentioned methods are being abandoned due to the inherent defects in them. These methods do not help in stock rectification since their approach is through Accession Numbers whereas the books are generally arranged subject wise and so it can not be found out easily as to whether a particular book was shelved at its proper place.

This method of stock verification presupposes the maintenance of an up - to - date and accurate shelf list on cards. If it is in register form, it will not be handy and the problems of Accession Register methods will recur to some extent. The card form is flexible and ensures speedy stock - verification. In this system, proper arrangement of shelf list cards is essential otherwise lot of time will be wasted in tracing out the exact titles. These cards, besides having the necessary information which is given for a main entry of a book, must contain some columns for recording stock - taking entries.

The particular drawers are taken to the shelves and the person on the shelves speaks out the call number of each book and the person with shelf list checks the call number. After tick marking the relevant year column goes on pushing forward the cards which have been checked. The cards bearing those a call numbers which are not spoken

0251.1 N242	Narayana, G.J.	
5492	Library and Information Management. New Delhi : Prentice Hall of India Private Limited, 1991, 307 p, 22 cm.	

1994	1995	1996	1997
1998	1999	2000	2001

Specimen of Shelf List with Special Columns

out by the person on the shelves are made to stand on their shorter edges and each day a list of standing cards is prepared after these cards are checked from other sequences such as those of the issue counter, binding, withdrawals etc. These cards represent those books which are not traceable. This list of books is got written off and proper remarks are given in the Withdrawal Register. The shelf list cards of the withdrawn books are filed in a separate sequence called withdrawal sequence.

This type of stock - taking is efficient and speedy but because one column is to be tick - marked on the shelf list cards, it takes some time. Moreover, the limited number of columns can be drawn on the face of the cards, so these cards become useless after some years and necessity arises for preparing fresh cards. If descriptive cataloguing is in vogue, it is difficult to provide such columns on the shelf list cards.

6. Stock - Taking By Shelf list Cards without Special Columns

This system is almost same to the previous one except that no specific columns are provided for tick - marking. Simply, the cards are pushed forward as soon as the call numbers of their respective books are spoken out by the person on the shelves. The cards of those books which are not found on the shelves are made to stand on their shorter edges and are marked with soft lead pencil. These cards are listed in the evening after these are checked with the charged trays, binding and withdrawals sequences and then the standing cards are put in their normal position. The specimen of shelf list card is given on next page be employed to do this job at one time. Moreover, since the books and cards are in one and the same sequence, checking is easier. The final is again checked with the shelves and those books which are found there are crossed from the list.

0251.1 N242	Narayana, G.J.	
5492		Library and Information Management. New Delhi : Prentice Hall of India Private Limited, 1991, 307 p, 22 cm.

Specimen of Shelf List without Special Columns

Besides, today are available many softwares like Libsys etc., which have the provision of stock-verification. If a library has been made automated, the stock verification can be done with the help of computers.

Stock Rectification and Stock Verification

The above mentioned methods dislocate normal circulation work. It is experienced that doing the entire checking at high pressure in a few weeks results in much dislocation in the work of the library. The dislocation will increase with the size of the library. The modern spirit, of library service has led the library profession to give up the old practice of closing the library for checking purposes."

Dr. S. R. Ranganathan has suggested a new system for stock taking purpose. He says that stock rectification and stock verification processes should be combined. In an open access library, though the readers are directed not to shelve the books by them selves, yet it is found that books are very often misplaced. A misplaced book is at least temporarily lost. Moreover, selfish and criminal minded readers do resort to such practices. They hide the books where nobody can ordinarily reach. For example, a student of 'Economics' may hide a book of Economics in 'Useful Arts' Section. A student of 'Economics' is unlikely to look up the section of 'Useful Arts' for his book on 'Economics' and so, for him, the book in question is temporarily lost. Second and Third Laws of Library Science are thus, violated. The importance of regular stock rectification cannot be overemphasized. Stock verification itself becomes easier and speedier if the books are placed at their proper places as indicated by the arrangement of the shelf list cards. He further suggested that this work should be done in a phased programme. The work of the Circulation and the Maintenance Sections should be so combined that proper stock - rectification and stock verification goes on smoothly. In this way, lot of time is saved. Moreover, if this method is followed, the library need not be closed for the readers.

For successful implementation of this method, the classification scheme in use should be such which provides individualized class / call numbers so that each book is identified by reading the class / call numbers only.

For the purpose, the whole length of stacks is divided into convenient parts and each part is allocated to a party of two persons. It is estimated that about 25,000 books can be rectified and verified within one month's time. One person goes to the Counter and asks the Counter Assistant to read out the Call Numbers of the books of particular region selected for checking for the day out of the Charged Tray. The cards of books not found out of this sequence are made to stand.

In the meantime, another staff member is asked to rectify the shelf pertaining to books to be checked for the day. The person who had gone to the Counter for checking comes to the shelves and asks the other person to read out the Call Number from the spine labels of the books. He himself goes on pushing towards himself the cards of the books, the Call Numbers of which are called out by the person on the shelf. At the end of the day's appointed quota, the cards of books of which the Call numbers are not called out by the person on the shelf are taken out and are placed in the Investigation Box. The cards which were made to stand on their short edges are turned to their normal position.

The cards in the Investigation Box are then checked with the Bespoken or Reversal Book Sequence, Binding Sequence and the books which are waiting to be shelved. The cards of the books which are thus found out are replaced in the Shelf List Cards Tray as usual. The remaining items are reported to the Librarian.

Now-a-days, ready - made software's are available in the market as library etc, which support stock verification also. Using software, a database of books etc. is created in the libraries. The accession numbers of books present in the libraries can be inputted manually or with the help of data - capturing unit (DCU). This data match automatically with the bibliographic database and the list of missing accession numbers with other details comes out.

Steps to Check Losses

The following steps and measures may be adopted in libraries to minimise the losses :

(i) Only one gate for ingress and outgress is kept open for the library visitors.

(ii) Throughout the opening hours of the library one janitor should always be on duty for checking the outgoing books and not allowing any book to pass from the library gate without its proper entry in the library issue records.

(iii) No personal property except notebooks or scrap book be permitted to be taken inside the library premises and for keeping the personal belongings of library users separate pigeon holes be made available near the entrance gate.

(iv) All the doors and windows of the library except entrance gate be covered with thick wire nettings.

(v) Brown System popularly known as Ticket System, one of the most scientific and standard system for maintaining records for circulation section should be adopted.

(vi) Besides following Brown system popularly known as ticket system for issue and return of books as a counter - check of outgoing books token system may be introduced. For each book issued to a member a token is given and the same is collected by the janitor at the library gate while allowing a book to pass out of the library premises. At the end of the day the three records namely the token register record, the issue record maintained at the circulation desk and the number of tokens collected by the janitor at the gate are tallied and any discrepency detected in records in immediately looked into.

(vii) The aforesaid procedure undoubtedly maintained, a check on the outgoing books but no counter - check is made of incoming books, i.e. books returned back to the library. Mere relaiance on the record maintained at the circulation desk is not enough. A double record for books returned to the library may also be kept in this system, one record is maintained as usual with the counter staff and the other separate record is kept by one senior technical staff member. A book on its return to the library has to be cleared at two places; firstly at the circulation desk and afterwards at the place; where duplicate issue record is maintained. The time taken in returning the book by the student is not the least affected by this procedure as the students card is immediately released by the counter staff.

(viii) All rare and expensive books particularly those with coloured plates and pictures should be kept in close access.

(ix) Wicket gate under the control of issue counter incharge should be provided at the exit of the library issue counter so that only one person at a time may be allowed to pass through it.

(x) To check pilferage and mutilation of books, convex lenses serving as magic eyes may be install at strategic places inside the library reading rooms and stack and through which the library staff may watch the movements and activities of library users by sitting at their own desk.

(xi) Closed circuit T.V. and cameras can be installed in the various sections of the library particularly reading rooms and stock and through them, the Librarian and senior staff may watch on the movements and activities of library users all the time, with least possible supervisory staff.

(xii) Library facilities to its users may be increased :

(a) By providing sufficient number of textbooks and books in great demand by readers.

(b) Book bank or Text Book Loan facility should be made available to students.

(c) Separate Text book Reference Section facility should be provided to students.

(d) Book Reservation System should be introduced in all libraries.

(e) By adopting procedure through which the library users could be informed immediately about the person to whom a book might have been issued and its due date should be devised so as to minimise the frustration of the library users.

(f) Photo - copying or Xeroxing, micro-filming and CD search facilities etc. at nominal cost should be provided to library users.

(g) Adequate Reference and Bibliographical services should be rendered to the clientele.

(h) Inter Library Loan facility should be made available at libraries.

(i) The library should observe extended library hours particularly during examination periods its doors should be open to users at least 12 hours a day and it should be open on Sundays and on most of the holidays.

(j) Library staff should be most courteous and cooperative with the library users and work with a missionary zeal and spirit.

Advantage & Disadvantages of Stock Tacking

Since every action has got some good or bad points, now the question arises whether in the present context it is desibrable to do stock verification every year as a ritual or completely abandon it as is being done in American and British Libraries. There are both good and bad points for both the views. According to E.R. Carbett, R.L. Mittal, P.K. Banerjee and others, Stock Verification has following advantages and disadvantages.

Advantages

1. It makes possible to bring the catalogues and other records uptodate, thus improving the reservation and Inter - Library Loan procedures and reducing irritation to both readers and staff.

2. It may reveal large scale losses and suggest additional security and precautionary measures.
3. It permits a general overhaul of the book stock and its physical condition and thereby old and damaged books lying on the shelves can be got repaired, written off or replaced by new copies of the lost titles.
4. It clears up many of the "quarries" which be set even the best run libraries.
5. Books are properly arranged on the shelves and the misplaced books are restored to the current places.
6. It satisfies the auditors and authorities that stock is being properly controlled.

Disadvantages

1. It takes up a considerable amount of staff time which might be better employed.
2. It's results are largely negative and unreliable.
3. It is virtually impossible in large libraries.
4. It causes unnecessary inconvenience to library users by closure of library or disruption in normal library activities and facilities.
5. Innocent library staff is put to unnecessary harassments by library authorities and some times it is used as an excuse for taking vengeance from certain staff members due to some past grievance or ill - will against them.
6. The amount of labour, time and money involved in stock taking is not worth the trouble as the monetary loss revealed by stock taking results is generally very meagre as compared to the overall expenses incurred by libraries on it.

Q. Explain the need for a binding policy in libraries. What are the contents of binding policy? Also discuss routine works of binding.

or

Discuss the purposes and objectives of binding and preservation of library materials. Describe the various steps of binding processes.

or

Differentiate Mending, Repairing and Binding. Discuss purpose and objectives of binding of library material.

Ans. Old books or manuscripts are very useful especially for research purpose. Special precautions should be taken for their preservation. The mending and repairing processes imply the following.

1. **Mending :** Minor restoration not involving replacement with any new material or the separation of book from cover.
2. **Repairing :** Partial rehabilation of a worn volume, the amount of work done being less than the minimum involved in rebinding and more than maximum involved in mending.
3. **Reinforcing :** Strengthening the structure of weakened volume usually by adding material.
4. **Recasting :** Replacing the cover on a volume which has come out its cover or has loosened in its cover, the sewing and cover, being still in good condition.
5. **Re-backing :** Attaching a new shelf back on a volume without any other binding.
6. **Resewing :** The process of making a new cover and attaching it to the volume.
7. **Recovering :** The process of taking out the volume out of its cover, removing the old sewing and replacing in the same cover.

Where as, the Book binding is an art of arranging, fastening together and carving sheets of paper composing a book, including ornamentation and decoration of the cover. It is the act or process of binding a book, whereby the sheets are sewn or otherwise fastened into a permanent cover of book binder's board, the sides and back of which are covered with leather or cloth, or other suitable material.

Objectives and Purpose of Binding

The purpose of binding is the preservation of written records. Whereas the main objective of binding is to build strength into a book, subjected to the rigorous and abuses of library usage. Binding ensures the preservation of written, printed or near print material. The other objectives of library binding are:

(1) to enhance the life span of library materials by insulating against wear and tear.

(2) To improve the durable quality of library materials i.e., maintaining them in good shape while being used, and

(3) To improve their aesthetic qualities by creating a new book and thereby attracting readers to them.

Quality of Good Book Binding

(1) Durability : The durability depends upon the raw materials - paper, cloth, thread, board, glue etc. used in book binding. The board should be selected according to the weight of the book. Sewing work be done properly by skilled hand or machine.

(2) Flexiblity : The binding of books be done in such a way that it does not create any problem or difficulty in opening the pages and reading the printed materials. The seqing and pasting work be done very carefully so that the printed matter is read without pressing the inside pages. Necessary precautions be taken so that the adequate margins on printed are left after sewing and edge cutting and the joints of the front and back cover remain flexible.

(3) Attractiveness : After rebinding the book must present an attractive look. For this every raw materials used in the binding be of superior quality and of attractive colour. There are several factors which help in presenting attractive look, like good pressing, proper gluing, backing and suitable cover.

Types of Library Binding

Most libraries acquire various kinds of materials which need differential handling and care. The question is that, what is an adequate programme of conservation and binding?

Binding does not present a serious problem when library materials are not used heavily, where periodicals are not kept permanently and where special materials are not collected. A library need not bind every item it acquires, however, every item should be maintained in such physical condition that it can be used by patrons without injury to the material. Neglect of binding activity in libraries would result in issues of periodicals getting lost or mutilated, books being used beyond repair, rare volumes being needlessly damaged, leather bindings being allowed to deteriorate, and special materials being destroyed.

The following binding styles are suggested as appropriate with the type of books mentioned. Its strain will depend on the expected amount of use and length of life of the particular books.

1. Heavily used reference books:
   (a) Large size - Half leather, Buckram or good cloth.

(b) Smaller size - Half leather, Buckram.

2. Less used reference books:

   (a) Large size - Full buckram.

   (b) Smaller size - Good cloth or rexine.

3. Little used reference books: Cloth or rexine.

4. Volumes of periodicals

   (a) Larger size - Buckram.

   (b) Smaller size - Good cloth.

5. Newspaper

   (a) Less than 2-1/2" thick - Buckram.

   (b) More than 2-1/2" thick - Half leather.

6. Pamphlets - ¼ cloth. Boards covered with strong papers.

   (a) Standard non-fiction -Good cloth

   (b) More ephimeral non-fiction and fiction - cloth or rexine.

Binding Policy

The main thing to keep in mind of binding documents are the type of material in terms of their physical quality and content value and extent and nature of use. All materials do not necessarily need the same type of binding in all libraries. Estimates of their useful life and of the extent of use that will be made of them, will help determine the best policy.

The following principles should be taken into consideration while taking a decision about the binding: (i) The physical condition of the book; (ii) the permanent value; (iii) whether it will be cheaper to replace a new copy than to bind. The standard reference books and other books which are in demand be bound without any loss of time. But other books which are not in demand and replaceable be kept aside. The rare and useful books deserve careful treatment. It will not be wise to make expenditure on an outdated, heavily, damaged, and incomplete books.

The selection of good book binder is another vital matter. The selection should be based on the reputation, experience and skill of the bookbinder. All the binders are not good to be library binding. According to *Louis N. Feipel* and *Earl W. Browning*, six classes of binderies are found:

(i) *Edition binderies* in which books are bound in quantity for publishers.

(ii) *Trade binderies* in which binding work is done for a printer.

(iii) *General job binderies* in which old jobs of binding either for the customer direct or the trade are performed.

(iv) *Pamphlet binderies* in which newly printed sheets of pamphlets or magazines are stiched, with thread or wire in large quantities for publishers.

(v) *Blank book binderies* in which ledgers and other book keeping and accounting volumes are bound.

(vi) *Library binderies* are binderies that are properly staffed and equipped, that specialize in the binding and rebinding of books and other printed matter of public and private libraries.

In the market a number of book binders are available and out of them a Librarian should be based on the following points:

(i) Class 'A' in materials and workmanship.

(ii) Dependable service.

(iii) Ability to abide by the agreement made between the Librarian and the bookbinder.

(iv) Best possible care in handling and protection of the books kept for binding at binders shop.

(v) Low cost.

Both the Librarian and the binder should try to establish and maintain a friendly business relationship.

Standards for Library Binding

In 1935 the American Library Association issued its 'minimum specification for Class A Library Binding' followed in 1939 by its 'Standards for reinforced (Pre-Library Bound) New Books' issued with the Library Binding Institute. These standards have been combined and have been revised as needed, to reflect new materials and new processes by the Library Binding Institute.

These standards which are useful are given below:

(i) All books shall be careful collated before being taken apart to detect any missing or damaged leaves or any peculiarities of paper or constructions that might take rebinding inadvisable.

(ii) All tears through print shall be mended with Japanese tissue or onion skin bond, and all tears in margins which bond paper of suitable weight.

(iii) Books unsuited for over sewing shall be prepared and reinforced through their folded sections.

(iv) Books that are to be oversewed shall be divided into uniform sections, each section not to exceed .050 inch in thickness, except flexible pulpy paper which may be thicker sections not to exceed .606 inch each.

(v) All end papers shall consist of three functional parts: apaste-down or outward end-leaf which becomes the cover lining; at least two free-leaves, and reinforcing fabric.

(vi) The construction of end papers shall be such that the sewing will go through the reinforcing fabric the same as through the sections of the book.

(vii) Most books having proper inner margins and suitable paper shall be sewed with thread by oversewing method, either by machine or by hand. If sewed by machines, all sections shall be pasted. No oversewing shall exceed 3/16 inch from the back of the edge of the volume and no nearer to the head and tail than ½ inch.

(viii) All books shall be trimmed as slightly as possible.

(ix) Edges shall be sprinkled, stained or left plain as instructed.

(x) Backs of books shall be glued with approved flexible glue, well rounded and backed, and lined with approved canton flannel extending to within ¼ inch of head and tail of books and well onto each end paper, approximately 1½ inches.

(xi) Covers shall be made of heavy weighty starch-filled or pyroxylin-filled buckram or drill base pyroxylin-coated material of a quality at least equal to the standards set forth in part v of these specifications.

(xii) Covers shall be made cover hard-rolled binders board, with uniform squares, in a neat manner. The thickness of the board shall be suited to the size and weight of the book.

(xiii) Books shall be cased in with glycol paste and pressed between metal-edged boards until thoroughly dry.

(xiv) Lettering shall be done after proper sizing in clear tape of a size appropriate to the book in style and position as instructed, using X.X.23 carat gold deeply impressed to insure long adhesion to the cover.

(xv) All books shall be sprayed or treated with a protective material evenly and lightly applied over their lettered backs.

Successive Operations in the Binding

The binding of books is both a craft and an art, although the artistic aspect has receded to the background in modern binding, except for some special categories of books. In the binding of book there are variations in its technique but the general pattern of processes in binding book by hand is fairly consistent. The basic patterns that have influenced all classes of book binding today, are as follows :

(i) **Collating :** To check all the books to ensure that all pages and plates are in their correct order, before the actual binding commences. It is a simple but important operation.

(ii) **Pulling :** Pulling or pulling down means stripping the old covers of a book, separating the sections, and removing the old glue prior to binding.

(iii) **Gathering:** Collating the sections into the correct order followed by attaching plates and mending tears.

(iv) **Pressing:** Solidifying the book by pressing between the two plates and leaving under a light weight until quite dry.

(v) **Marketing Up:** Lines made on the spine indicate the position of the tapes or chords on which the book is to be sewn.

(vi) **Sewing:** One section after another is sewn on the tapes or chords. The lines sewing thread trend from end to end of each section until the whole section is sewn.

(vii) **End Paper:** Pasting together stout, white or coloured sheets for lining the insides of the covers and protecting the first and last leaves of the book. The end papers are sewn or pasted on the book.

(viii) **Fraying Out Slips:** After the book has been sewn the cords are cut so as to leave an inch and a half or so overlapping, and these overlapping pieces of cord and known as slips. Fraying out slips means separating and softing with paste the ends of the cords coming out from sides of sewn sheets.

(ix) Gluing Up: Application of glue to the spine of a book after sewing but not very thick glue. This consolidates the sections and makes it possible to mould the spine in its slight rounded shape.

(x) Rounding and Backing : Rounding is the process of moulding the spine into shape. Backing is the action of hammering the spine, after it has been sewn and had its first coat of glue, with a round headed hammer. This process can be done by machine also.

(xi) Lining the Board: Lining up is necessary for producing a smooth surface of the spine so that the finished work can be carried out effectively. A piece of material usually 'mull' placed in spine of a book when binding it to give its strength.

(xii) Cutting in Boards: The boards are cut in size either by a cutting machine or by shears screwes up in a 'lying press'. The plough is used cutting straight and square boards.

(xiii) Lacing in Boards: The boards are attached to the book by threading the frayed out chords, to holes near the joints.

(xiv) Knocking Down the Swelling: The increased thickness of the back of the book due to the strand of thread inside each section is known as the swelling. If this is slight it can be left to the rounding process, but if excessive it must be reduced by slightly imbedding the thread in the paper. For this knock up the book square at the back and head between the boards with the tapes outside the board.

(xv) Pressing and Cleaning Off: After attaching the boards the book is placed in a press with tin plates on each side of the board and is left there overnight. This helps to solidify the book. The surplus glue is scrapped before it becomes dry.

(xvi) Edge Cutting: The top, fore and tail edges of a book is cut solid by guillotine machine which possesses a knife having a perpendicular action.

(xvii) Edge Gilding and Colouring: The edges of the paper are treated in one or other fashion. Gilding involves the process of applying red chalk paste on the edges by dipping the brush in the mixture and the gold may be sprayed softly and be dried under normal temperature. This work can be done after cutting the boards.

(xviii) Fixing Head Band: Head bands serve as a decorative function on machine and craft binding and then glued to the head and tail of the spine. Now a days, headbands are made of coloured silk threads and are sown on after the book has been forwarded.

(xix) Lining Up: The spine of a book is lined with a piece of paper or leather when binding it to give it strength.

(xx) Binding: When the sewing has been recessed, small strips of leather are glued at cross spine. These when covered with leather will provide the raised bands.

(xxi) Paring: The leather inteneded for the cover is thinned at certain points. This enables it to be turned in neatly where necessary particularly inside the cover, and by this method proper finishing is attained.

(xxii) Covering: The bound books are generally covered with paper, or leather, or cloth. The material is cut with the required size, is pasted and then folded on to the book.

(xxiii) Trimming: The leather on inside on the board is trimmed, so that the margin is equal all round.

(xxiv) Tooling: Spine is lettered with the title, name of the author etc. and any other gold decoration or lines required are added before gold leaf can be applied to a book. It needs a medium to hold it and this medium is called glair.

(xxv) Polishing: When the book is completely lettered and decorated the surplus gold is rubbed off with a hot smooth iron or a soft rubber. This gives an attractive appearance.

(xxvi) Final Pressing: Finally, after complete of all operations of binding, the book is pressed for atleast 24 hours.

Routine Work of Binding

The routine work of sorting, preparing and despatching books to the approved book binder should be entrusted to an experienced and intellegent staff who could do the work with sincerity. Before despatching the books for binding the staff entrusted with this work must know about the sanctioned budget amounts so that the total expenditure incurred under this need not exceed.

Duties and responsibilities of the binding section be mentioned as follows:

(i) Forward the proposal with full justification to the librarian for provision of annual amount in the budget for binding work.

(ii) Collect the damaged and worn out books and to prepare a list of such books with style of binding, lettering etc.

(iii) Preparing the binding order slips for each item to be bound. In each binding order slip the columns for informations about Name of the Library, Style, Colour, Price, Binder, Title, Author, Call No.and other instructions are given.

(iv) Move for selection of suitable binding.

(v) Negotiating with binders concerning rates, standard of materials, workmanship and time to be allowed.

(vi) Entering into agreement with the binders before awarding work.

(vii) Maintaining binding records.

(viii) Establishing close co-operation with acquisition, circulation, technical, periodical, and account section.

(ix) Keeping control over expenditure.

(x) Checking the quality of work after receiving back the books from the binders. Any discrepencies be reported to the bindery firm.

The Librarian or his senior deputy supervise the work of this section. In this way the work of this section will give better and satisfactory result.

As soon as the verification is over the bills of the bound volumes should be forwarded to the accounts sections for payment. The accounts section will then check up the rate and amount etc. from record and the final payment will be made. The bound volumes will then be transmitted to the maintenance section for placing them at their appropriate places.

3

Library Finance: Budgeting and Accounts

Q. : Explain scope and principals of financial management for libraries.

Ans. The word 'finance' is used to express any statement of monetary accounts or comparison of income with expenditure. Finance is the life-blood of any institution or of any firm. It is essential for effective functioning. Financial management is a diagnostic technique for detailed analysis of future oriented activities of persons and groups of persons responsible for administration.

Some guiding principles are necessary for effective financial management. These are:

(1) Effective Control

(2) Simplicity

(3) Regularity and Farsightedness

(4) Economy

(5) Flexibility

(1) Effective Control : Financial management can work efficiently only when it is controlled properly. The method of financial control should be simple and easy. Control is also necessary for the economical use and chanelisation of resources so that there is little wastage and the limited financial resources can be put to maximum use.

(2) Simplicity : The procedures for financial management should be simple and easy to operate. Simplicity results in efficiency and economy.

(3) Regularity and Farsightedness: Financial management programmes should have a typical timetable so as to acquaint everybody with what he/she is expected to do at a particular point of time. For example, in the preparation of the budget for a library, inputs should come from the heads of sections who would in turn expect cooperation from their staff. The preparation of the budget would be time-bound and the budget should be submitted to the authorities on time so that the budgetary sanctions can be obtained in time to operate it. Similarly subscriptions to current journals should be sent to the publishers at a particular time of the year. Sticking to a timetable facilitates advance thinking and preparation. Not only present needs but future requirements should be kept in view when making provisions for finance.

(4) Economy: Economy should be effected in any and every activity, more so in financial matters. All precautions should be taken to avoid unnecessary expenditure and wasteful use of scarce finances.

(5) Flexibility: Financial management should keep in mind the virtues of elasticity so as to learn scope for adjustment according to circumstances. Only then can it be successful in times of emergency and crisis. But this does not mean that one should take undue advantage of its flexible nature. There are provisions and practices in utilising or diverting funds appropriated for a certain item of expenditure to the purchase of books or any equipment. But this flexibility should be within the framework of financial rules and procedures. This type of adjustment usually is done at the fag end of the financial year when unutilised funds are available in other items.

These principles are useful in operating and managing finances in libraries, but there are statutory financial rules and procedures laid down by the executive authorities. Libraries have no option but to follow financial rules.

Q. : Discuss the various sources of finance for an academic or a university library.

Ans. Sources of finance means what are funding sources of libraries. Inspite of variation in nature, type and locality of the libraries, a library usually has following sources of income:

* Government grant
* Library tax
* Donations and endowments
* Library fee
* Late Fee or Fines

* Miscellaneous
    * Sale of wastes, used news-papers etc.
    * Library publications
    * Interest from bank on fixed deposits
    * Rent from library property
    * Income from different programmes

As far as the university libraries are concerned, in India, main source of finance of universities is government grants that may be provided by respective state government or central government, and sometimes by both. It depends firstly on the nature of university and secondly the funding plans of government. On the basis of funding agencies we can divide universities in 3 types -

(a) Central Universities : These are funded by Central government (Ministry of Human Resource Development) through UGC.

(b) State Universities : For maintenance grants they depend on the state government but they also get some special grants from UGC under various schemes.

(c) Private Funded Universities : Though in West, most universities are privately funded universities, but these are now started in India also. There are also some such universities, those have been provided with the status of "deemed universities" but they mostly look at the centre or state government for funds. They send different plans which if approved, get grants from state or central government.

The gate-ways open for universities to meet financial situation which seems inevitable are as under :

1. Self financing

UGC suggested universities to raise their own finance. Education in India is a social welfare activity but now the concept seems to be changing slowly. It will give way to the privatisation of education. Concept of free library services is vanishing and marketing of library services, like in the West, will start. Actually it has already started in case of different computerised and on-line services. INSDOC and DESIDOC are imparting some such services on payment. Similarly academic libraries should also charge for special services.

2. Fees and fines

Almost all university libraries charge fees from their students for its use but it is so meagre that it cannot be considered as a dependable source of finance. This is because, charges for education in India as compared with West are very low. In West, education is available to all but charges are so high that everyone cannot pay for it, so one who can pay it, can get education. But in India fees had been stagnating for nearly last 50 years which is quite an unrealistic occurance.

The fines are charged in library for late return of books or against losses or misuse of books. But it is not enough to be considered as a source of finance, because its main aim is to compel the user to return the borrowed books in time and not to damage it.

3. Self - paying education

Many institutions were charging capitation fees which were banned by Supreme Court. They have introduced new scheme of 'self-paying' education which has now got governments' approval. Similarly libraries may launch special schemes it they want to improve their economic health.

The following sources of income of university libraries are the major sources:

(i) Funds allocated from the university budget
(ii) Grants from foundation of another agency
(iii) Endowments and Gifts
(iv) Caution money
(v) Miscellaneous sources

(i) Funds allocated from University Budget

The financial demands of universities are of two types viz.,

(a) Recurring grants
(b) Non-recurring/Ad hoc grants

The recurring grants are given generally for the purpose of purchase of books and periodicals, maintenance of regular services and for anticipated contingent expenditure. The non-recurring grants are given for specific purposes e.g., for preparing special collection, purchasing equipment and furniture etc.

In India central universities get different grants from central government i.e., Ministry of Human Resource Development through UGC. The state universities depend for maintenance grants on the state government, But they also get different types of grants directly from UGC or other central government agencies like CSIR, ICSSR etc. These provide finance for establishing collections for a newly started department. The other source is equipment grants e.g., UGC is funding universities for purchasing computers to establish local Network and later become part of INFLIBNET. Besides, UGC also gives non-recurring grants for construction of library buildings etc.

(ii) Grants from a Foundation or Another Agency

The grants from a foundation or another agency can be a useful source of revenue. Under the Wheat Loan Programme of the United States, India received $ 1,70,000 during the first eight years beginning with 1954, for the purchase of American books and exchange of librarians. Many university libraries have received large grants from various foundations, especially from Ford Foundation, the Asia Foundation and the Rockefeller Foundation. In 1967-68, the University of Delhi received a Ford Foundation grant of $ 351,000 for library purpose for a period of three years in the first instance. It received in 1961, a grant of $ 177,475 and of Rs. 58,250 from the Rockefeller Foundation for the training of teachers of library science, getting consultations, acquiring reading materials in library science and equipment etc. These are the grants received by some selected libraries for a short duration of period.

(iii) Endowments and Gifts

An endowment is a permanent means of support, but the university libraries cannot depend on these. Some libraries were really benefitted from the Ford Foundation, Rockefeller Foundation and PL 480 (US government's funds under India Wheat Loan Programme) funds etc. but all these were temporary help and supported very selective libraries only. Truly speaking these are not very common in India.

The libraries may encourage passing out students and research scholars and retiring and desirous teachers to donate their books to the respective library which will prove to be a great help to them. But libraries should make a policy to receive only such books which are of permanent use, otherwise they will increase their problem instead of enriching their collection. Problem in they sense that the will occupy the space and create shortage of space and money will be wasted on staff, maintenance etc. on that trash material.

(iv) Caution Money

Many libraries receive caution money from its readers. It is refundable and refunded when a reader ceases library membership. But its interest becomes a handsome source of income.

(v) Miscellaneous Sources

Alongwith the above sources of finance libraries have some more areas of making funds. The following are the miscellaneous sources :

(a) Sale of Library Publications : A library may have a publication programme. These publications may include bibliographies, indexing services, abstracting services, handbooks, guidebooks, periodicals etc. If a library is an active one it can have a publication programme on a large scale.

(b) Sale of Waste Papers : Sale of old newspapers, magazines, pamphlets, written off books, etc. can be a small source of revenue.

(c) The libraries do charge subsedized rates for translation and reprographic services but now they should raise their charges, of course, not equal to market rates, at least to meet the maintenance charges of these equipments etc.

(d) In some universities, prices recovered for lost books, for lost reader's tickets, unclaimed library security (if any) are transferred to university funds which should be treated as library income.

Besides, the commission taken on the purchase of books can also be taken as the source of income, which can be utilized for some purposes in a library.

Q. : What is budget formulation? Discuss its various steps in details.

or

What are the methods of financial estimations? Explain the need for budgetary norms and standards.

Ans. Budgeting being an economic process, one has to put its plans and proposed programmes into an economic format. Some of the factors associated with formulation of a budget are :

1. Methods of Financial Estimation

Proper financing is possible on the basis of correct and effective estimation of finance. These estimates are always made for the coming year. The financial requirements of a library depend on the following factors -

(a) Age

(b) Jurisdiction

(c) Quantity and quality of reading material

(d) Number of readers

(e) Number of research scholars

(f) Seating capacity

(g) Staff and

(h) Services provided by library

There are various ways of financial estimation for calculating the financial requirements of an information institution. The most popular ones being followed in India are.

(i) Per Capita Method : In this method, a minimum expenditure per library user is fixed which is considered essential for providing standard library and information services. To determine the per capita finance of the information institution, the factors taken into account are the cultural and educational standards of the society, the per capita income of the society, the average cost of published documents, the future needs of the information organization and the salary of the various personnels working in the information organization. At times, the per capita estimate can also be based on the number of registered borrowers of the institution. However, the best way of calculating the library finance is to take into account all the users of the library irrespective of their level.

The per capita figure must be calculated keeping in view the rising cost of documents and revised after every few years. The University Grants Commission Library Committee has recommended that a University Library should provide Rs. 15 for each student and Rs. 200 for each teacher for buying reading material in academic libraries. Dr. S.R.Ranganathan had suggested a per capita expenditure of Rs.20 per student and Rs.

300 per teacher for college and university libraries. For public libraries, he had suggested Rs. 50 per capita expenditure.

But all these norms were laid down by back in 1950s and 1960s. Now the per capita income became much higher as per prevailing costs and it should be revised accordingly.

(ii) Method of details : According to this method of financial estimation, all items of expenditure of an information institution are accounted for while preparing the estimates. Here both the recurring or current expenditures and non-recurring or capital expenditures are taken into account. This method is quite authentic and detailed but does not reflect the changes if any to be included in a fresh budget.

(iii) Cost of Additions Method : In the cost of additions methods, the total financial estimation is on the basis of the cost of the documents that are to be added every year. This method also aids the library's plan which projects the total number of documents which are expected to be added at the end of each year. Although quite useful, this method is helpful only in organizations where data on the total annual expenditure is not available.

(iv) Method of Proportions : In this method, the financial estimation is based on the principle that the certain minimum percentage or proportion of the whole budget incurred by an organization has to be allocated to its library or information centre for the annual expenditures.

Various standards for deciding the proportion or the percentage of the total budget have been recommended by various authorities.

UGC's Party committee (U.K) suggested that 6 percent of total university budget may be provided to university libraries in U.K. Radhakrishnan commission recommended that 6.25 per cent of total budget of a university be provided to its library. The Kothari commission recommended provision of 6.5 to 10 per cent from university's budget for library, depending on the stages of development of the university. But usually, it varies from 6 to 10 percent of the total expenditure depending upon the size, type and objectives of the parent organization of the library/information centre.

2. Foundations for creating a Budget

As budgeting is an economic process, one has to put its plans and proposed programmes into an economic format. To this in the most convincing fashion, it is important that one should have a sound grasp on some of the basic economic concepts as they relate to decision - making. Some of the basic economic concepts include :

Sunk cost - It is basically anything that has already been spent and is irretrievable.

Opportunity cost - Those costs involved in the opportunities foregone in the pursuit of the alternative that has been chosen.

Investment decision - It is the decision to propose spending some resource - time, money or effort for some future advantage or benefit.

Net present value - It is a concept for making money expended or received at different times comparable with each other.

3. Justifying a Budget

The most fundamental concept to be kept in mind when preparing a budget is its later defense and justification. The library/information manager has to adopt certain techniques that allow the ready budget to be justified before the higher authorities. One of the most popular techniques includes using a programme budget concept as this identifies what you are trying to accomplish, what the programme of the institution are and what are the costs for each of these programmes.

The other justification techniques are - the tier or the incremental approach, padding, use of standards, performance figures, quantification and graphic presentation. Besides the above the best way to get the budget approved, is to be honest and straightforward with the higher authorities during the budget presentation.

4. Foundations of Cost Analysis

The most convincing presentation of a budget is most often based on an underlying cost analysis of different alternatives. The ability to prepare a sound and convincing cost analysis is, therefore, basic to good budgeting. Some essential aspects of cost analysis are :

Allocation - It is the process of assigning costs to programmes or outputs.

Direct costs - A cost element that is specifically and conveniently linked to a particular work output.

Indirect costs - Costs which cannot be directly attributed to particular work outputs and are, therefore, assigned to these outputs on the basis of some rational decision rules.

Joints costs - The fact that different programmes or outputs may have expenses allocated to them from the same joint costs.

Fixed cost - It is a cost which does not change in total within a reasonable range of operations.

Variable cost - A cost which fluctuates in total in direct proportion to changes in the level of production.

Q. : What do you mean by library budget? Discuss the methods of preparation a budget for an academic library?

or

Distinguish Zero based budgeting and Performance budgeting with suitable examples?

or

Discuss Zero-based budget with its advantages and disadvantages.

or

What should be the attributes of a Library Budget? Describe the practical procedure for preparing budget for a library.

Ans. The term 'budgeting' refers to the process of budget planning and preparation, budgetory control and the related procedures. The formal presentation of the plan is called budget. Budget is a written statement of income and expenditure during the year. It covers all items of work to be taken up over a specified period of time in future. Thus an overall budget covering the institution as a whole is also known as 'master budget'.

The primary purpose of budgeting is to provide an opportunity to examine the composition and viability of an institution's resource base for each programme and activity.

The development of budget should ensure that all institutional activities and programme are examined simultaneously to determine, in light of available resources, which one should be supported and to what degree. The process should communicate the institution's priorities to various constituencies, identify specific commitments, and establish preliminary control over its resources. The result of this process is a plan that is used to monitor and control the institution's ongoing operations.

There are two types of budgets :

* An operating budget, which is a financial plan of current operations that encompasses both estimated revenues and estimated expenditures for a specified period and
* A capital budget, which outlines expenditures for new construction, major repair or renovations, and major items of equipment, often for a specified period of one or more years, depending on budget requirements.

A library budget is an estimate of expected income and expenditure of the library for the coming year. Being merely an estimate, it can be altered, due to change in the circumstances. It is usually done on yearly basis.

Preparation of budget takes a great deal of time. Generally, during the middle of a current financial year, budget estimates for the next financial year are called by the office of the parent body. The librarian is expected to submit the budget estimates in the proforma approved by the institution on the basis of the past experience, present demands and future expectations of requirements.

Objectives of Library Budgeting

The overall objective of library budgeting is to plan different phases of library operations, Co-ordinate activities of different departments of the library and to ensure effective control over it. Thus specific objectives may be outlined as follows :

1. To predict library's future services, service costs and other costs to achieve desired goals.
2. To anticipate library's future financial condition and the future need for funds with a view to keeping the library active and uptodate.
3. To co-ordinate the efforts of different departments of the library towards the common objectives.
4. To accelerate the efficiency of operation of different divisions and departments of the library.
5. To fix responsibilities of different departmental heads.

6. To have effective control over the library's funds.
7. To facilitate centralised control over the library through the budgetory reports.

Budget Affecting Factors

Budget may be affected by the factors mentioned below :

* Size of the library - collection, staff, users and service points.
* Location.
* Kinds of library services.
* Types of users.
* Rising costs.
* Period covered (one year or more).

Budget Techniques

There are a variety of ways in which budget may be prepared and presented. The major approaches which are in use today are being described here.

* Line-item budget
* Lump sum budget
* Formula budget
* Performance budget
* Programme budget
* Planning programming budget system (PPBS)
* Zero-Based budget

1. Line-item Budget

Line-item budget is the most commonly used kind of budget. Each line is increased a little each year. No questions are asked.

Here the items of expenditure are divided into the broad categories as given below:

Items	*Revised budget for 2002-03*	*Proposed budget for 2003-04*
Salaries and wages	Rs.400,000	Rs.420,000
Reading materials such as books Periodicals etc.	Rs.20,000	Rs.220,000
Equipment	Rs.10,000	Rs.10,500
Binding	Rs.10,000	Rs.10,500
Heating, lighting, water and telephone	Rs.10,000	Rs.10,500
Stationery, printing and supplies	Rs.4,000	Rs.4,200
Insurance	Rs.10,000	Rs.10,500
Miscellaneous	Rs.10,000	Rs.10,500

The current budget is prepared, increasing each item over the previous year's allocation. The increase may range from 5 to 10 percent. The salaries and other items are increased by 5%, keeping in view the minimum of 5% rise in general prices. Prices of reading materials have gone up by 10% as the library acquires a large number of reading materials published abroad. The authorities would understand the reason for increase in the allocation of each item.

In this kind of budget, there is no relationship between the request made and the objectives of library. The reallocation of funds can be done provided the authorities agree in this regard.

2. Lump-sum Budget

In lump-sum budget, a certain amount of money is allocated to the library. The library is given the necessary freedom to decide as to how the amount is going to be allocated to different categories. The apportioning of the budget is responsibility of the person handling the information institution.

3. Formula Budget

Formula budgeting is used to allocate the distribution of funds to various organizations performing a similar or parallel function. For example, the state, may distribute funds to libraries within the state university or college system based upon the same formula. The formula could include some factors such as the number of undergraduate students, the number of postgraduate students, Masters level programme, Ph. D. level programmes, the number of faculty etc. Such a formula can be designed to allocate a precise number of rupees to determine the proportionate percentage of the whole sum which each institution will get, within the overall amount sanctioned for the whole institution.

A formula budget determines how much money the individual library is going to receive. And it will be still up to the library to determine how to spend the money. Therefore, the formula budget provides guidance for the individual library as to how the money might reasonably be spent.

4. Performance Budget

In performance budgeting, the organization's budget is based upon developing unit costs for the activities that the organization carries out. The emphasis is laid on the efficiency of operations. The quantitative data about all activities is collected carefully over a period of time. The management techniques like cost benefit analysis are applied to measure the performance. The norms are established. For instance, one can determine the manpower, money and materials required to carry out classification and cataloguing work. However, this would require expensive and complicated techniques.

A performance budget looks very scientific and has a certain surface validity in that it looks convincing and plausible on the surface. It is also somewhat more sophisticated than a line item budget. It does allocate costs such as salaries and telephone charges to the different activities being undertaken - circulation, processing and reference etc. It does not, however, explain to administration the purpose of the activities.

5. Programme Budget

It is concerned with activities. The amounts are allocated to programmes or services rendered. In programme budgeting, the proposed expenses of the organization are analysed and delineated in terms of the functions that the organization undertakes, i.e., its programmes. An organization's programmes can, of course, be analyzed and dissected in many ways. Budget preparation guidelines formulated by the organization may include a programme breakdown, but it is more likely that the librarian will make that analysis. In programme budget the library's proposed expenditures are set forth as they relate to different programmes.

The principal advantage of the programme budget, if it is clearly presented, is that one can see what money expended is doing; what is intended to be accomplished with that money, and where it is going from the point of view of the organization's goals. One can also more clearly see what will suffer if the budget is cut or, in more hopeful circumstances, what resources will be needed to increase the scope or extent of any particular service or function.

6. Planning Programming Budgeting System

Planning Programming Budgeting System (PPBS) is a technique, which takes into consideration the best of programme budgeting and the best of performance budgeting. Here the focus is on planning. The important steps in PPBS are:

(a) to identify and list all the objectives of the information organization;

(b) to present alternative ways to achieve the objectives listed above with their detailed cost benefit ratios;

(c) identification of the activities necessary for each programme;

(d) evaluating the result in order to take corrective action if any required.

The PPBS thus, combines the functions of planning activities, programmes and services, translating them into tangible projects and finally presents the requirements in budgetary terms. The table given on next page, gives data about a college library. The library serves 1000 students and 50 teachers. On an average 200 books are issued and returned per day.

7. Zero-Based Budgeting (ZBB)

ZBB is a method of budgetary planning and presentation which includes objective setting, programme, evaluation and operational decision-making, involving managers and staff. It requires that the cost of all programmes, both current and new, be justified at the beginning of each budgetary cycle. In each fresh budgetary cycle, the previous sums appropriated are 'set to zero' and each proposal is justified afresh.

The first step in the implementation of ZBB is the identification of "decision units" Decision units are the basic components of the organization's operations. They may be programme, projects, services, etc. The major step in ZBB is the creation of a decision package of each programme of decision unit that is proposed. The decision package

Input-cost	*Kind of Service*	*Objectives of the Programme*	*Output totals*	*Cost per output*
Rs.25000 (Salareis, cost of equipment, stationery etc.)	Lending service	Lending of documents for home use	24000 documents	Rs.1.04
Rs.15000 (salaries, stationery, etc.	Cataloguing and Classification	To classify documents and prepare catalogue cards, filing of catalogue cards, stamping and pasting	1200 documents	Rs.12.50

Example of PPBS : Use of Lending Service in a College Library for the Period, March to August, 2002

describes the programme, project or operation that is to be undertaken, the rationale for undertaking it, the benefits, impacts, ramifications, and of course, the costs. These various impacts and benefits should be quantified as much as possible. In addition, the decision package should reflect alternative methods for accomplishing the same goals and give the reasons for rejections the alternative. If more than one alternative remains, the costs, benefits, ramifications, etc. of these alternatives, as far as they are feasible, should be compared.

The second and final step in ZBB, is the ranking of the decision packages. After the decision units have been decided upon and the packages have been created and assembled, they are evaluated and ranked by the next higher level of management, either for final decision making purposes or they be combined and reassembled as necessary to create decision packages for the next higher level of management.

With these decision packages in hand, determinations are then made as to how to allocate the organization's resources. The principal advantage of the system is that resources can be matched to programme in a rational fashion. If expenditures must be reduced then the inclusion of alternative levels of support in the various decision packages allows for a decision as to where money will be cut back, with some understanding of what the impact of that decision will be. ZBB thus allows for much more rational allocation of resources. It has other benefits also as the budget is tied to the goals of the organization. The organization's programmes and activities reflect its goals more closely. ZBB also improves the provision of information to management. On the other hand, the management knows in much greater detail as to why the money is being spent and what options are available if changes need to be made. Finally, ZBB if properly implemented, develops increased involvement of personnel at all levels.

Problems in ZBB

When ZBB is introduced, three types of problems can be expected:

(i) **Fears and Administrative Problems** : Managers are often apprehensive of any process that forces decision making and requires detailed scrutiny of their functions; administration and communication of ZBB in large organizations is very difficult; first year time requirements may exceed the time spent in prior year's planning and budgeting.

(ii) Decision package formulation problems : Determining the activities, functions to develop decision packages; subjectivity in judgement in establishing the minimum level of effort; identifying work measures and evaluating data for each activity; costing of decision packages etc.

(iii) Ranking process problems : Determining the person who will do the ranking; evaluating dissimilar functions, especially when subjective judgment is required; handling large volumes of decision packages, etc.

It can be concluded that, in spite of the problems, one may encounter in ZBB, it facilitates justification of budgetary requests. This is because of the fact that ZBB involves the identification, evaluation and justification of all activities proposed. In addition, it is very good resource allocation tool for the managers as it provides consolidated ranking of activities. Further, due to its analytical and yet integrated approach facilitates elimination of duplicative efforts. So it must be remembered that ZBB is a tool an cannot be considered as a panacea to solve all management problems. Nevertheless, it facilitates decision-making, especially in the allocation and utilisation of organizational resources.

Tips for Successful Budget Making

1. A general budget file should be maintained containing all the details.
2. Each section can maintain their budget file. Necessary additions can be added to it and then recommendations are given and incorporated to the main budget.
3. It should be based on object classification.
4. Departmental reports should be incorporated in a general budget form.
5. Accounts assistant should carefully do the calculations.
6. Probable income should also be checked.
7. The net amount required should be struck down by bringing out the difference between the estimate expenditures and income.
8. The budget estimates should be framed carefully.
9. Ways and means should be suggested for procuring additional revenue to meet the deficit.

Q. : Write a short note on an Ideal Budget for a library.

Ans. The main heads for which funds are required are - documents (including books, periodicals, and other forms of reading materials), staff salaries, services, building maintenance and miscellaneous expenditures on telephone, stationary, transport, postage, etc.

The allocation of funds to various heads varies form library to library. As per the different standards suggested by different experts, about 40-50 % usually goes to salaries of staff, about 30-40% on documents and the rest is spent for maintenance and miscellaneous expenditures.

The allocation of funds to various heads in kind of libraries too varies. For example in academic libraries, more amount on books is required whereas the public libraries require more for staff salaries and maintenance and the special libraries spend more on documents other than books and on services. In this connection, DR. S.R.Ranaganathan has suggested a formula wherein 50% of the total budget is for staff, 30% for books and the rest for maintenance and miscellaneous expenditures. In the present day context, this formula and norms need to be raised as many of our procedures are automated and moreover DR. Ranaganathan's formula is over four decades old.

An ideal budget thus, should have the following percentage of allocation to various heads for different types of libraries.

University Library

Salaries and wages	40%
Documents	30%
Services	10%
Maintenance of Building	5%
Miscellaneous	15%

College Library

Expenditure on reading materials	36%
Staff salary	50%
Binding	4%
Others	10%

Public Library

According to Ranaganathan, the annual recurring expenditure on public library system will be:

Staff salary	50%
Cost of reading materials, binding, and other Expenses	50%

Note: Experience shows that 25% be spent on reading materials, 5% on binding, others 20%.

Special Library

The budget for Special Library may be as under :

Expenditure on reading materials	35%	(2/3 on periodicals and 1/3 on books)
Staff salary	50%	
Equipment	9%	(1/4th of expenditure on reading Materials)
Other expenditure including binding, distribution of documentation list etc.	6%	

The individual library should not restrict itself to any formula in toto but as per needs and demands of its users the budget allocation should be made.

4

Organizational Structure; Library Personnel : their Classification, Qualification, Job Analysis, Staff Manual and Human Resource Development

Q. : Explain the need for an organizational chart of a library?

or

Describe the organizational structure of a university library with the help of an organizational chart.

or

Describe the principles of organizing that are helpful in creating an efficient organizational structure in a library.

or

Explain the various characteristics of division for organizing the activities and programmes of a large library.

Ans. Human resources are important for success of any organisation as people are the key to the effective and efficient functioning of any organization. The planning process establishes clearly the defined goals and objectives of any organisation. This leads to the beginning of the function of organising. For organising the functions of a library, its activities relating to each function have to be divided into works and jobs and group and arranged to form a structure. So it is a practice to divide and group the activities of a library into desirable sections/units for getting best management results. Some suitable characteristics should be determined for division which would be relevant to fulfil the purpose. The following characteristics are now being used for creating sections/units in a Library.

(a) Numbers, (b) Functions, (c) Territory (geographical contiguity), (d) Product, (e) Customers (users), (f) Process or Equipment, (g) Subjects, (h) Materials (books, periodicals, microfilms/forms, maps, etc).

The most common form of organisational design is the functional structure. This divides a library into functional departments/sections/ units such as-Acquisition, Technical, Processing, Circulation, Reference, Documentation, Extension, Maintenance, etc. The academic libraries use the criteria 'subjects' which provides for more-in-depth reference and information services, requiring a higher degree of subject specialisation on the part of the staff. In academic libraries, subject departments are usually broad in scope to include all related subjects.

Principles of Structuring

In the process of designing the organisational structure of a library, the dividing and grouping various library activities produce a number of horizontal and vertical units at different levels. So these units need to be structured relating them approximately, to produce a desirable organisational structure for effective administration and efficient management. This structure is essentially an establishment of appropriate relationship between various groups of persons working at vertical and horizontal positions of a library. Therefore, it is necessary to adopt some useful principles for creating organisational structure such as:

(1) Span of Management : It refers to the number of activities a manager can effectively manage. This emphasises on the limit to which a Librarian/Information Officer would be able to supervise, control and manage a number of activities efficiently.

(2) Scalar Principle and the Vertical Hierarchy : It needs that there should be final utilise authority and the lines of authority should clearly extended downward to every subordinate position in a library.

(3) Unit of Command : It emphasizes that each employee is supervised by only one supervisor who should make assignments and asess the employee's performance.

(4) **Delegation of Authority and Responsibility** : It states that responsibility can not be delegated without accompanying authority. The process of delegation should consider certain facts such as:

(a) assignment of tasks,

(b) the determination of the results expected,

(c) degree of delegation of authority for performing the tasks,

(d) exact fixation of responsibility for failure or success in performing the tasks of an employee in a library.

(5) **Line and Staff Positions:** Line positions or managers are responsible and accountable for the tasks assigned to them in the achievement of organisations' aims and objectives. Staff positions are those that provide advice, support and service to the line positions/managers in carrying out their tasks. Usually staff positions are created in big libraries to streamline operations on the basis of advice give to make right choice from different alternatives.

(6) **Functional Authority** : It relates to supervisory power exercised on a section/unit by a position/manager/specialist outside the organisational section/unit. In libraries, often functional authority is given to specialists who complete a particular project work within specific time. Sometimes, they are known as co-ordinators because they have to work with employees involved in their type of speciality.

(7) **Co-ordination and Integration:** The employees of a library work in different positions to accomplish the desired result but these positions are not to be operated in isolation. So they have to operate in close cooperation and coordination with various units of a library. Thus, the final integration of different functions alone will ensure success.

(8) **Centralization and Decentralization:** In a library, certain activities need to be centralized and certain others decentralized. But a judicious combination would ensure best results in most economical way. Therefore, in big libraries, house-keeping operations may be centralised and specific services may be decentralised.

Library Organizational Structures

Organizing involves determining the specific activities necessary to accomplish the planned goals, grouping the activities into a logical framework or structure, assigning these activities to specific positions and people and providing a means for coordinating the efforts of individuals and groups. Organising thus divides activities into manageable units and makes each unit's work compatible with all the others. Organising determines the way by which the goals conceived in planning can be accomplished. It can be viewed as a bridge connecting the objectives developed in planning to the specific means for accomplishing these objectives.

One of the most important aspects of organisation is choosing the design of the enterprise, both the structure or the organisation and the allocation of the jobs. It the work of an organisation is to be carried out by one or two persons, there is no need to organise, but as soon as an organisatin grows, more persons are required to work, decisions must be made about its organisation.

The two key concepts in organising are specialisation and coordination. Each organisation must decide how it wants to divide its tasks or specialise, this specialsation involves breaking the whole organisation into parts and each part of department carries out some specialised activity. Coordination on the other hands involves informing each worker about his area of activity to avoid confusion and duplication of effort.

Organisational chart

An organisation chart is a useful visual aid for including the horizontal and vertical structure of an organisation. It is a graphic presentation of organisational structure showing different positions, span of control, relationships between line and staff positions, flow of authority and responsibility, relationship with advisory committees and such others.

It is important for each type of library to have an organisational chart irrespective of its size. In case of large libraries, organisational charts should be prepared very carefully and they are very helful in day to day functioning of the library. While preparing organisational charts, the following aspects should be taken into consideration:

(a) size of an organisation

(b) flow of authority and responsibility

(c) horizontal and vertical positions

(d) span of control

(e) functional and coordination aspects

(f) status of staff members

(g) lines of communication

The organizational charts reveal that a library, its staff and the external environment exist in a complex and interwoven relationship. Organising provides techniques for structuring these relationships in a meaningful manner, that is for establishing relationships that provide the best flow a activities, ideas, authority and responsibility. Order and clarity arise from organising.

Below are given, two charts for College Library and University Library respectively.

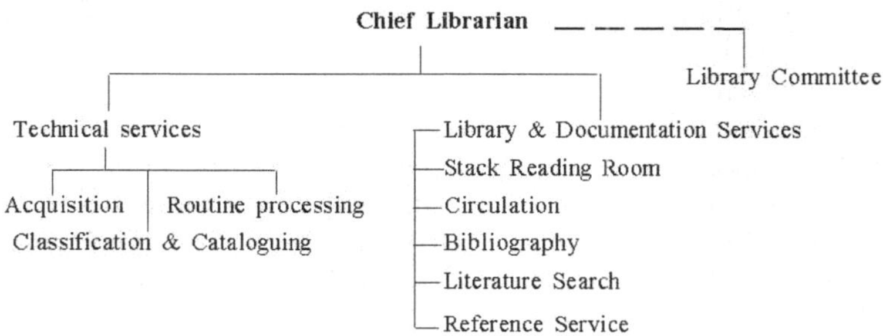

Fig. 1. Organisational Chart of College Library

In first chart, the main authority starts with Chief Librarian, which also acts ex-officio secretary for library committee. Then, all services comes under the Librarian only supported by supportive staff.

In case of a university Library. The main line of authority flows from Chief Librarian, which continues upto various sections of the Library headed by junior administrative staff. While interpreting organizational structure, it is very essential to know that from where authority flows out and stops on which points.

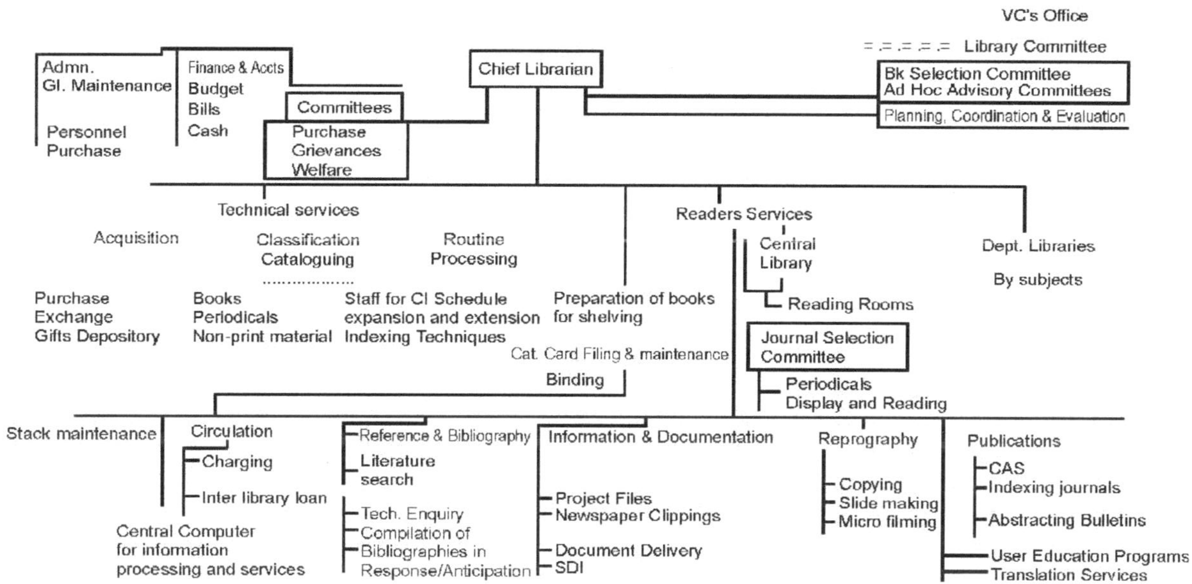

-.-.-.-. Relation with the Authority
- - - - Relation with Advisory Committees
Hierarchical Relationships (line relationship)
.... Staff relationships

The journal selection committee may comprise persons from Acquisition, Periodicals, Reference & bibliography and Information & Documentation and Publication Divisions. There are many junction points, which have not been indicated in the chart.

Fig. 2. Organisational Chart of a Large University Library

Q. : Discuss the staffing pattern of a library

or

Discuss University Grants Commission formula prescribed for staff strength for a University and College Libraries.

or

Write short notes on followings:

* **Staff Manual**
* **Classification of Library Staff**
* **Job Analysis**
* **Professional Qualifications of the Librarian**

Ans. Staffing is the function concerned with the employment and training of employees, and maintenance of conducive environment, for accomplishing the objectives of an enterprise.

Once the structure of the organisation is finalized, the next stage is to define the actual duties allocated to each individual and to ensure that as far as practical the group of duties allocated to each person is a fair quantity of work for him or her to perform. In this connection, job analysis, categorization of staff, their recruitment and staff - manual for staff, are the various steps to be followed for proper management of a library. These are discussed one by one.

(i) Job Analysis

It involves the analysis of the contents of each job to be performed in an institution. Job analysis finds out what is to be done and determines the best method of doing it, and the qualifications required of a worker to be able to do the job satisfactorily.

The data to be obtained should be comprehensive and reliable. It should be accurate. The data should include: the specific activities, responsibilities, special information needed by the employee, how the work to be performed, working conditions and physical demands.

Once the job-analysis is completed, then prior to going, for recuritment it is essential to categories the staff and to determine the numbers of staff to be recurited.

(ii) Categories of Library Staff

Manpower is the most vital and powerful of all the resources of any information organisation. A library can have an excellent collection of documents, plenty of online resources and a beautiful and comfortable building, but if it does not have a well-trained, competent staff, the users using the library will not be served properly. It is therefore essential that every library is staffed with the persons with good academic background, professional knowledge, competence and a service attitude.

According to nature of work, the library staff can be divided into following categories.

* Professional staff
* Semi-professional staff
* Non-professional staff
* Supporting staff

(a) **Professional Staff :** With the increase in range of specialised services in libraries, it has been essential for all kinds of libraries to employ personnel who can perform professional duties. The professional staff should have sound academic background, professional knowledge, required skills and a service attitude. Professionals usually involve themselves in intellectual and non-routine activities which require their academic background and professional expertise. They also play leadership roles, directing the various divisions of the organisation and provide the specialised expertise to fulfil the information needs of the users of the library. They constitute the top and middle level of management holding positions like the Chief Librarian, Director, Librarian, Deputy librarian, Assistant Librarian, Professional Assistants, etc. In other words they form the core of any library to achieve its objectives.

(b) **Semi-professional Staff :** In every library, there are activities which are of routine or repetitive nature. These are performed by professionals who have some library training that prepares them to handle all kinds of routines in a library. The also pick up skills while working on the same job for a number of years and are competent to handle all the routines efficiently. This category of staff are referred to as Semi-Professional as they can effectively carry out the routine professional duties assigned to them. Some of these routines include shelving, charging and discharging, preparing publications for binding, typing and filing catalogue cards, claiming non-receipt of periodical issues, searching books on the shelves, tooling the books, etc. All these jobs, although are simple, require good understanding of library activities and services on part of the persons handling them.

The staff members in this category, belonging to middle or lower level of management, are referred to as library assistants, technical assistants, cataloguers or shelf assistants and provide the required support to the higher levels of management.

(c) **Non-professional Staff :** The library also has a number of jobs related to financial and administrative matters. These include purchase of materials, acquiring stationery and equipment, maintenance, engineering works, security, cleaning, financial matters, typing work, etc. Although these are routine work, personnel with specific skills are required to handle each activity. The number of personnel to be employed in this category depends on the size and kind of library. In many cases, these personnel belong to the parent organisation of the library and handle the library work too. They are referred to Administrative officer. Finance/Accounts officer, Section officers, Office assistants, Accounts assistants, Typists, System analysts, Secretarial staff, etc.

(d) **Supporting Staff :** Modern day technologies have led to the increased use of computers, communications and media technologies for providing efficient library services. Every library requires personnel for carrying out the following jobs:

* Handling of audio-visual materials,
* Computer applications for various housekeeping operations of the library that include acquisition, processing, cataloguing, circulation, etc.,
* Computerised database creation, data entry,
* Networking activities,
* Reprographic services especially photoduplication of library materials,
* Publication activities, i.e. Desk Top Publication activities for printing lists, etc.

All the above activities require electronic equipment and handling of which involves skilled personnel. A library may have to employ network administrator, system analysts, database administrators for handling various computer related activities. For handling audio-visual materials and reprographic equipment, trained persons are to be employed who can keep the machinery and equipment is proper order all the time. This category of personnel work in coordination with the professionals and semi-professionals and are very essential for smooth functioning of any library. They are thus referred to as support staff. They usually belong to the middle or lower level of management.

(iii) Staff Formula

While job analysis helps to decide the type and quality of staff of library with reference to its functional requirements, its staff size has to be assessed in terms of analysis of its work load. Man hours required to complete a targeted volume of work with in a time frame has to be worked out according to a standard staff formula with reference to the certain parameters, which would help assessment of the size of staff required.

There is no universally acceptable standard staff formula available, meeting all requirements and conditions, for determining staff size for a library. The another way is to say that size of staff depends upon or varies from library to library. However, Dr. Ranganathan has prescribed a staff formula for Indian Libraries which is a useful guide. Staff formula for every activity in a library has not been given, but many of the conventional functions in library is included in his prescription.

Ranganathan's staff formula for

(A) Professional Staff : SB + SC + SL + SM + SP + SR + ST

(B) Non-Professional Skilled staff : B/30,000 +(S/100)

(C) Unskilled staff

SB/4 + SC/2 + SL + SM/4 + SP/2 + SR/8 + A/20,000 + D/500 + B/60,000 + S/100/4 + V/30,000

Where,

SB = Number of persons in book section

SC = Number of persons in circulation Section

SL = No. of persons as Librarian & his/her deputies

SM = No. of persons in maintenance section

SP = No. of persons in periodical section

SR = No. of persons in reference section

ST = No. of persons in technical section i.e. Cataloguing & Classification section.

B = Annual Budget allotment in rupees

S = No. of seats for reader

A = No. of volumes accessioned in a year

D = No. of periodicals abstracted & Indexed in a year

V = No. of Vol. in the Library

G = No. of gate hours for a year

It may be noted that requirement of staff for each section has been calculated on the basis of experience.

SB = A/6000

SC = G/1500

SL = HW/1500

$$= \frac{\text{No. of hours library is kept open in a day} \times \text{No. of working days in a year}}{1500}$$

SM = A/3000

SP = P/500

$$SR = \left(\frac{R}{50}\right)\left(\frac{W}{250}\right)\left(\frac{\text{No. of readers per day}}{50}\right) \times \left(\frac{\text{No. of working days in a year}}{250}\right)$$

$$ST = \frac{A + 40D}{2000}$$

The following staff formula has been restated by Dr. S.R.Ranganathan for different kinds of libraries:

(a) Public Libraries - for Professional Staff

S. No.	Section	Public Library
1.	Book Section	One person for every 6,000 volumes added in year
2.	Periodical Section	One person for every 1,000 volumes currently taken
3.	Technical Section	One person for every 2,000 volumes added in a year
4.	Maintenance Section	One person for every 2,000 volumes added in a year and one person for every 50,000 volumes in the library
5.	Publicity Section	Minimum one artist
6.	Administrative Section	Minimum one library accountant, one steno-typist and one clerk
7.	Reference Section	One person for every 50 readers using the library in a day of the year
8.	Circulation Section	One person for every 1,500 hours for which one counter is open
9.	Supervisory	One Librarian and one Deputy Librarian

(b) University and College Libraries : Formula recommended by the library committee of University Grants Commission (1957), of which S.R.Ranganathan was the Chairman:

S.No.	Section	University and College Library
1.	Books	Same as for Public Library
2.	Periodicals	One person for every 500
3.	Technical	Same as for Public Library
4.	Maintenance	(a) One person for every 6,000 volumes added in a year (b) One person for every 500 volumes to be replaced in a day; (c) One person for every 1,00,000 volumes in the library

5.	Documentation	One person for every 1,000 entries prepared
6.	Reference Section	Same as for Public Libraries
7.	Circulation Section	- do -
8.	Unskilled Staff	One attendant each for 60,000 volumes added in a year, for every 500 current periodicals taken. One cleaner for every 30,000 volumes in the library.

Staff for publicity section has not been provided for University and College libraries.

Qualification of Library Staff

University Library Staff : The minimum qualifications for appointment to the posts of Librarian, Deputy Librarian and Assistant Librarian/Documentation officer according to UGC letter of 20th Feb.1990 are given below :

(A) Librarian (University)

(i) Master's Degree in Library Science/Information Science/ documentation with at least 55% of the marks of its equivalent C.G.P.A. and consistently good academic record;

(ii) At least 13 years as a Deputy Librarian in a University library or 18 years' experience as a College Librarian;

(iii) Evidence of innovative library service and organization of published work.

Desirable : M.Phil/Ph.D. degree in Library Library Science/ Information Science/Documentation /Archives and Manuscript-keeping.

(B) Deputy Librarian

(i) Master's Degree in Library Science/Information Science/ documentation with at least 55% of the marks of its equivalent C.G.P.A. and consistently good academic record;

(ii) Five year's experience as an Assistant University Librarian/ College Librarian;

(iii) Evidence of innovative library services, published work and professional commitment computerization of library.

Desirable : M.Phil/Ph.D. degree in Library Library Science/ Information Science/ Documentation /Archives and Manuscript-keeping, computerization of library.

(C) For the Posts of Assistant University Librarian/College Librarian/Documentation Officer

Minimum Qualification

(i) Qualifying in the national-level test conducted for the purpose by the UGC or any other agency approved by the UGC

(ii) Master's degree in Library Science/Information Science/ Documentation or an equivalent professional degree with at least 55% of the marks or its equivalent C.G.P.A. and consistently good academic record, computerization of library.

Note : The NET qualification is relaxed for those who are M.Phil by 1993 and those who had submitted their Ph.D. thesis upto 2002.

(iv) Recruitment and Selection

The recruitment of library staff is to be planned properly. The main aim of recruitment should be to secure best candidates for performing specific job in a library. Proper recruitment presupposes an efficient system of dissemination aimed at informing the prospective candidates about the vacant jobs in library. This information should include the salary scale, allowances, fringe benefits, and working and service conditions attached with the jobs. The future prospects of the jobs and the profession of librarianship should also be brought to the notice of the prospective candidates.

Selection refers to the process of actually choosing the individual who will be most likely to perform successfully in a job. The primary purpose of selection is to achieve a good match between the qualifications and experience of the candidate selected and the requirements of the post. The successful matching of candidate to a post is very important because wrong selection will only create problems to the library.

The library should have a well designed selection system that will work to select persons best suited to the requirements of a job. The selection process, generally, includes analysis of the data obtained through application forms, selection tests, personal interviews, verification of past performance and background of the selected candidates and finally issuing the appointment orders.

If a test is to be held as a first step in the selection process; the following aspects need careful attention

* Criteria for eligibility for the written test of the applicants,
* Kind of test to be held, choice of examiners, evaluation criteria, etc.,
* Preparation of the question paper and evaluation of the answer scripts,
* Listing of successful candidates for final selection through personal interview,
* Fixing the dates for the selection committee meeting and conducting the interview.

(v) Job Description

Job Analysis leads to Job Description which implies the recording of the following data concerning each job analysed:

1. Principal duties to be performed and responsibilities involved are outlined.
2. Operations involved in each job are listed in proper sequence.
3. Requisite materials, equipment, machinery and tools etc. are listed.
4. Conditions of work i.e., surroundings, the time of work etc. are stated.
5. Relations of various related jobs are indicated.
6. Mental and physical abilities for performing each operation are listed. The kind of training and the length of experience required are also indicated.
7. Wages payable alongwith other fringe benefits are stated.

(vi) Staff Manual

Manual is a book that gives information or practical instructions. Library manual gives guidelines to the staff of the library as to the sections, levels of staff, their functions, work-flow, records to be maintained, coordination among staff, preparation of reports, etc.

It is advantageous to have a staff manual prepared for each library which spells out the various jobs and help as a guide for reference in the hour of need.

Such a Manual should give a detailed chart of various positions indicating coordination and subordination, line of control, job specification of each employee, etc. These manuals should also specify, the procedure for recruitment, qualifications, age limit and other service conditions as well.

The major areas that need to be specified includes:

1. **Job titles**
2. **Distribution of work** - Distribution consulting, Distribution communicating, Distribution reporting, etc;
3. **Work Assignment** - Casual jobs -Assignment consulting, communicating, assignment adjusting, etc.
4. **Discipline Work** - *Immediate jobs* - control of Class IV employees, Attendance watching, Reporting abnormalities; *Daily jobs*-Scrutining attendance register, Absence intimating, etc; *Weekly jobs* - Obtaining explanations for memos, Forwarding explanations, Transmitting decisions, etc; *Monthly jobs* - Writing attendance register, Work report of various employees ; Sectionwise-qualitative as well as quantitative.
5. **Time-Table** - Finalization, Reconciling, etc.
6. **Staff Order Book** - Casual jobs: Staff order writing, order circulars, instructions to new recruits, etc.
7. **Diaries** - Daily job of scrutinizing, intimating abnormalities, weekly and monthly totals' scrutinizing, etc.
8. **Junction Moments** - Watching, Adjusting if necessary, Avoidance of conflicts, etc.
9. **Progress Report** - Correspondence, Disposal of pending items, Rounding of routines.
10. **Accounts** - Financial diaries, Monitoring expenditure, Payments, Maintenance of accounts and correct figures etc.

Q. : What do you mean by Human Resource Development? Why it is needed in the libraries ? Discuss how it is implemented in a library?

or

What do you understand by staff development? Discuss briefly.

or

Write on essay on Training Programmes for the library staff.

Ans. Human Resources Development or HRD is a process of helping employees in an organization to acquire new skills and competence on a continuing basis. The organisation should provide facilities to the employees in a planned and systematic way to:

— acquire and sharpen skills and capabilities to perform various tasks associated with their present and expected future roles;

— develop their general capabilities, discover and exploit their inner potential for their own and/or organisational development purposes;

— help to bring about an organisational culture in which collaboration among sub-units is strong and contributes to the supervisor-subordinate relationships, team work and the professional well-being and pride of employees;

— facilitate upgrading of skills through mechanisms and instruments; and

— improve abilities by the introduction of strategic and operational HRD planning and execution.

Need of HRD

HRD, is necessary for any type of organisation for:

— survival and stability;

— growth and development;

— change and diversification;

— retuning the activities to become more effective;

— providing highest quality in products and services;

— playing a leadership role in the field; and

— obtaining goodwill and reputation through customer satisfaction.

Components of HRD

An HRD programme for an organisation is a planned activity. It should include a clear statement of objectives and goals, strategic and operational planning, and appropriate means, mechanisms and instruments for execution.

(1) Strategic and Operational Planning

Strategic and operational planning is largely confined to defining the objectives of the organisation, preparing policy guidelines, evolving pragmatic plans and strategies for executive actions, and establishing appropriate procedures, rules and regulations for implementation at all levels. This would ensure :

* professionalism ;
* personal involvement in work in achieving set targets;
* formalisation;
* enhancement of work skills ;
* increasing application of information technologies ;
* evolution of a corporate culture; and
* continued progress and development.

This approach would encourage organizations to plan their future staffing structures and to take into account changes in services and technology. Exercised properly, and on a continuing basis, it should eleminate problems of oversupply or undersupply of particular skills within an organization. It also aids the determination of training needs in relation to new skills required.

Operational planning would take care to implement and execute the activities and programms to achieve the targets set by the objectives and goals of an organization. Further, it handles personnel recruitment, selection, placement and deployment, and personnel skill development through training and hands-on experience. The distribution of personnel to the various units. Division and departments is done through task analysis, job analysis, job description, job specification, competencies etc. The implication of this exercise is that the right person should fit into the right job that would not only ensure work efficiency and quality but also give the concerned person job satisfaction.

(2) Implementation of HRD

The first step towards HRD is to set up a unit in the organization to deal exclusively with personnel development programmes. The mechanisms to implement these programmes are to introduce a process of performance evaluation of staff at all levels, assess deficiences or under performance, and such other shortfalls in performance. Corrective steps are to conceive and design specific instruments to set things right and get maximum productivity through the optimum efficiency of the staff. The HRD unit should concern itself with the following aspects:

(i) Performance appraisal : It is a periodical evaluation of employees' performance. Proper evaluation is carried out with appropriate yardsticks; data on performance review and feedback from the employee are estimated with reference to the employee's optimum potential. Performance coaching and counselling would enable employees to contribute to their optimum potential.

(ii) Role analysis : Role is the position an employee occupies as defined by expectations of different significant persons have for the person. Role analysis is concerned with optimum stress, linkages and autonomy. Optimum stress refers to tuning a person to raise his contribution to the optimum level. Linkages provide for intra and inter relations between individuals and teams within the units and outside. Autonomy permits an individual to display initiative in dealing with a new problem and finding a solution to it.

(iii) Training policies : These are widely laid down and practized in most organizations to build up staff skills. Training has to be with reference to the types of training required by an organization, in-house training or training by professional bodies or institutions, evaluation of trained employees and utilization of the training obtained.

(iv) Communication policies : This contributes substantilly to the health of the organisation. Through appropriate internal communication channels, the organisational activities can be authentically reported. This would prevent unnecessary faith in grapevine and gossip among the employees. The employees would also be properly informed about the activities and progress of the organization.

(v) Job rotation : Judicious transfer of persons to pick up experience and expertise in different areas of work in different units of an organisation is known as job rotation. This would also contribute to the health of the organization.

(vi) Organization development : An organization has to be dynamic and should positively respond to changes in the environment, advances in technology, and diversification of products and services. Growth, impact in the field and self-developing mechanisms are important for organization development.

(vii) Award, reward and incentives : Another important aspect relates to awards, rewards, incentives schemes, both for individuals and groups, which would generate greater involvement of employees in work and contribute to quality assurance. This scheme needs very judicious implementation, i.e., only after a foolproof method has been evolved. If this precaution is not taken, undesirable results detrimental to organizational growth may follow.

(viii) Organisational culture : For the development of an organizational culture, an appropriate environmental climate is necessary. Communication within the organization that permits top-down, bottom-up, horizontal, circular and external communication has to be built into the organization. This would ensure smoothness in employee-employer relationship. This would also create the right atmosphere to develop a work culture, contributing positively to the organization.

The above aspects would be influenced by factors like management style, environment, technology, resource availability, background and past history of the organisation, nature of business, and others.

If properly attended and successfully implemented, this is likely to be reflected in organizational effectiveness like higher productivity, growth and diversification, cost reduction, more profits and a better image of the organization.

(3) Staff Development

Staff development is similar to Human Resource Development (HRD) process. The difference is only that HRD is concerned with the development of human resources in the same cadre or capacity in which a person is recruited whereas the staff development is concerned with over - all ups of a person including his promotion and welfare. There are several aspects related with staff development. These include:

(i) Probation : Many authorities have a provision of probation for all new appointments. The period of probation varies from organization to organization and post to post. At the end of the probation period if a satisfactory report is received from the appropriate head of the department, the concerned member of staff is confirmed. If the report is unsatisfactory, the probation period may be extended or services of the person concerned can be dispensed with.

(ii) Appraisal : The probation system sometimes entails performance appraisal or called 'assessment' or 'evaluation'. These are also used for assessing eligibility of each member of staff at periodic intervals. The self appraisal report serves as a basis for rewarding who have rendered excellent service and the management makes use of his capabilities and potential for the interest of the organisation. Since such reports are confidential in nature and the authorities make use of this, it could contribute to achieving higher levels of staff performance.

(iii) Promotion : Promotion is one of the ways of staff development. It usually entails an increase in the salary, higher status, greater responsibility and other perquisites on the expectation that the individual has the skills, preparation and personality for success in the new job.

Besides the qualifications and past experience, annual confidential character roll (performance appraisal) for promotion, is taken into consideration partially on the basis of involvement in professional activities at the local, regional and national levels. Papers presented at seminars and conferences, offices held, awards received are also all taken into account. Participation in continuing education, involvement in research activity and contributions to books and book reviews are all granted a place in committee considerations.

(iv) Induction : Induction is aimed at familiarizing the newly recruited staff with the new surroundings, colleagues, organisation, place of library within it and the basic regulations involved. Thus, the newcomer will be given an introduction to his immediate supervisor and the staff with whom he is to be in regular contact, brief function of the department in which he is to work as well as other sections, introducting Library's union representatives, the conditions of service, working hours, leave, staff facilities etc.

(v) Training : Training is a continuous process involving experience and courses, both within and without the library which keep up with the constant changes in librarianship. This sometimes provides an opportunity to acquire an additional skill and leads to improved chances of promotion.

In terms of the library's objectives, the only real justification for money spent in training is that it should contribute to the aims and purposes of the service and that the same objective could not have been achieved in any cheaper way. The most useful way of ensuring that training is cost-effective is to utilize a framework.

The training may be sub-divided fourther into following types :

(a) In-service/job training : The most obvious training need for any employee is instruction and practice in the tasks comprising his job. Job training is a way of reducing expensive mistakes and accelerating learning on basic skills. The usual method is for colleagues, or immediate superiors, to instruct the new entrant in the manner known as 'Watching Nellie'. This casual approach can have drawbacks:-

(i) existing staff can pass on mistakes as well as experience;

(ii) not all staff are competent instructors;

(iii) traditional methods are not always best for present needs and rigidity of approach can result from such handed-down information.

On the plus side such training is the easiest, cheapest way of familiarizing staff with new tasks. Existing staff are knowledgeable about the job in the context of that particular library.

(b) Continuation/development training : As users' needs change so much library staff alter and amend the tasks they do and the ways they do them. Continuation training aims to develop new skills in all staff - both newly arrived and with more experience- to prevent any divergence of purpose between library objectives and the tasks designed to achieve them.

(c) Specialist training : Professional staff may develop interests in specialist library work. Examples are - reference service, childern's services, readers' advisory work; not everyone is clear about their special option subjects at Library School. Specialist training is beneficial to both the library and staff career development. Large systems, especially those with professional training officers, can run such courses in-house.

(d) Management training : It is not easy to pinpoint the stage at which management skills become necessary. The Librarian-in-charge of even the smallest library has a staff to deploy and a service to manage. The more senior posts, especially in large libraries, involve management of large staffs, stocks, and budgets and increasingly require professional management expertize.

Increasing size and complexity of library systems - and changes in the technology and products they employ - makes management training more and more necessary. The large management schools have been slow to respond to the needs of the public services, although now there are a variety of courses geared to a non-profit making sector. Another problem for senior librarians is that time away from work is hard to obtain - the very people who most need management training are the ones least able to be spared. Part time courses minimize the problem, at least as far as retention of a job is concerned. It does not alleviate workload, though, but adds to it and, for this reason, part time management courses are recognised as endurance tests in their own right.

(vi) Staff Records : An efficient system of personnel management presupposes that within any concern, a systematic record will be kept of every member of staff from appointment to resignation or retirement. All staff records should be treated as highly confidential and staff in charge of personnel matters should ensure that no unentitled person has access to such records.

(vii) Welfare : General welfare of the staff at all levels means both physical and mental well-being. Responsibilities of this nature need the co-operation of both the employers and the employed. The library authorities have a duty to ensure that adequate attention is given to staff working conditions and that potential sources of danger are elimited. Provision of fire regulations by installing alarms and fire extinguishers, emergency exists, emergency lights, steps and ladders, regular servicing of boilers, proper training to the janitors, lifts and hoists, polishing of floors regularly, keeping the library environment free from air pollution, chemicals and other similar hazards, adequate ventilation should be made available to the library staff to take adequate precautions against creating potentially dangerous situations for others through sheer carelessness and ignorance.

Thus, the HRD process complete for an organization including Library and Information centre.

5

Library Building : Planning, Furniture and Equipments

Q. : Describe the major steps in planning a Library Building in India, indicating the Librarian's role in this activity.

or

Discuss in detail the fundamental points, which you should be kept in view while planning for a Library Building.

or

Explain the role of Librarian and Architect in planning the library building.

or

Enumerate different points that you would kept in mind while planning a modern library building.

Ans. The process of organization of a library starts with the planning of its building. Irrespective of big or small, luxurious or plain, broad or tall, the library building must primarily be functional and it must suit the purpose for which it is planned and created.

The appointment of Librarian is the first step in the direction of planning of a library building. He will able to do the spare work necessary for planning and equipping the library. A brief note of the Librarian for the architect can be valuable in drawing the map of the building.

In the first place, the Librarian has to define the purpose which the library is being created to fulfill, and he has to identify the many and various functions which it has to perform, to show the relative importance of each and the relationship between them. Not least, he has to forecast the future, so that a library can be planned to service not only today's needs, but the needs of the next twenty, thirty or forty years. This is a serious and complicated task for which the Librarian must equip himself.

The Librarian's brief pertaining to the planning of library may contains the following information.

1. Activities of the library

   (a brief description about the functions and objectives of the library)

2. Clienteles

   (a) Regular

   (b) Potential

   (In case of the University and College library, the categories of users)

3. Automotion

   (i) Computer system

   (ii) Networking

4. Size of the library

   (a) Location

   (b) Site

   (c) Access

5. Space requirement

   (i) Stack

   (ii) Reading room

   (iii) Staff's room

   (iv) Seminar and meeting hall

   (v) For non-book materials.

6. Front Elevation

7. Interior design

8. Exit and control

9. Entrance and Gangways

10. Air-conditioning and Lightining

11. Equipments & Furnitures

12. Future Extension
13. Location of Different Sections
14. Librarian's and Deputy Librarian's Office

Library Building Planning

The planning of library building is a team work and a planning committee is to be formed to look ofter the matter of library building. Library authority or the management committee may form a team consisting of the Librarian, Engineers and the Architect. Following are some of the points to be kept in mind before going to construct a Library building.

1. Preplanning Activities : The pre-planning activities include gathering information including internal information, through visiting other libraries, discussing with colleagues and experts, attending seminars, exhibitions, conferences and reading literature. One should not be surprised or scared at issues cropping up, rather one should try to discuss with colleagues and experts. The proposal should incorporate general features like objectives, type, status and location of the library, nature of users and use of library, special construction features of the facility, statistics regarding existing library, resources required and the implementation schedule, etc.

2. Physical Facilities and Environment : The physical facilities and environment can be looked from three important view points, namely, marketing of services, quality of services and customer (user) studies.

Physical environment need to be improved for the following reasons and ways:

(i) customer judges the service quality through the process of deduction.

(ii) Creation of service environment (i.e., context) should not be left to chance.

(iii) Both dominant and peripheral physical evidences should be coordinated to achieve uniformity in projected service image.

(iv) Peripheral evidences are small to trival but have impact on customers.

(v) Perception about services are sources of competitive differentiation.

(vi) When it comes to perception "feelings are facts".

(vii) Help to reinforce the proposed position and image of the organisation, i.e., tangibile the intangible service through physical environment.

3. Clientele : The understanding of the users in terms of their characteristics, styles, idiosyncasies, needs, opinions, priorities, preferences, evaluations, attitudes and behaviour is essential. A number of findings in the areas of user research provide clear and direct input for creating appropriate physical facilities and environment. The type of library, nature of users, pattern of usage, age and status differences, psychological and behavioural patterns of clientele are to be given due consideration in planning a library building.

4. Location or Site : Location is important for homogeneous services, site selection and choice of community, region, etc., depend on the factors like convenience, operating cost, proximity to competitor, availability of support system, geographical or environmental factors like noise, traffic, communication networks, transport facilities, channels/distribution/service centers, etc.

Ideally, a library should be centrally located so that it is easily accessible to its clientele. It should be set up in serene surroundings, insulated from din and dust.

5. Budget : The budget also plays important role in preliminary activities. It is essential to know how much of the money is with us for constructing a building and what services we are going to provide. Whether the budget is sufficient for the purpose? If not what types of the services we may suspend for the time being and accordingly the building is constructed.

6. Finalization : After all the above consideration the planning is finalized. If all the members of authority/committee are satisfied, then the finance is arranged and construction of library building may be started.

Principles of Library Building Construction

The following principles are set for library building construction, which are to be followed during the construction of a library building.

(i) Functional Design : A library building should have functional design rather then a monumental one. Thus, functional requirements should get preference.

In begning, the university library building constructions were massive library structures, which gave an impression of monumentality. The factors which are important in a good library such as functionality and expansibility were not given much importance, however, in recent days, building constructions have taken into consideration these factors to a certain extent.

(ii) **Open Access :** A library building designed for open access system is also considered useful for a 'close access system'. Provision of 'open access system' has certain implications. There should be one entrance and one exit to keep a proper control on incoming and outgoing users. The height of the unit book rack should be such that a person of normal height should be able to pick up books from top most shelf.

(iii) **Future Growth :** A library building should be planned for at least next 10 years, keeping in view rate of stock development, number of readers, future use of microforms etc. The building should be extendable to allow for future growth with minimum of disruption.

(iv) **Flexible :** In case a change in library functions takes place, then it should be possible to adjust the layout without carrying out major structural operations. This means interchangeability of all major stack areas, service areas, reading areas and staff areas. There should be no interior loadbearing walls but building should be able to bear stack load anywhere. Uniform standards of lighting, ventilation and flooring are necessary to meet the criteria of interchangeability.

(v) **Provision of Areas :** There should be provision for documents, users, staff, service areas, library tools like public catalogue, microfilm reader, computers and xerox machine etc.

Mainly the following four broad areas along with their allied and sub-areas are identified as common service areas in a library :

(a) Circulation area, which includes :

  (i) Stack rooms or halls

  (ii) Charging Desk

  (iii) Public Catalogues

(b) Reader Activity Area, which includes:

(i) Reading rooms

(ii) Microform reading room

(iii) Study carrels

(c) Staff activity Area, which includes:

(i) Acquisition section

(ii) Technical section

(iii) Reference section

(d) Other Areas, which include :

(i) Senior professionals rooms

(ii) Space for library staff

(iii) Seminar room

(iv) Binding section

(v) Reprography section

(vi) Internet browsing section

(vi) Accessible : Building should be accessible from outside and from the entrance to different parts of the building by means of simple and easy to understand plan requiring only a few directions or guides.

(vii) Modular Design : The basic dimensions of library building furniture and fittings should be in multiples or submultiples of 10-cm module. This would be the case for tables, chairs, book racks, book trolleys, doors, windows, etc. The dimensions of dirrerent items should register with one another. A column spacing of between 22½ to 23 feet from centre to centre has been suggested.

A building based on modular system is the one supported by columns placed at regular interval. Only columns are loadbearing inside the building, however, outside walls may also be loadbearing, Columns, stairways, lifts, heating facilities, plumbing and ducts are all fixed and everything else is movable. Modular system leads to flexibility.

(viii) Economic : Design should be economical to carry out and result in a building which can be maintained with minimum of staff and the finance.

Besides, the lighting facilities should also be good. As for as possible, rooms etc are designed in such a way that natural light during the day time may come inside the rooms. The rooms and reading areas must also be well decorated to create a pleasant environment for continous reading.

Q. : What different kinds of library furniture and equipments are required in a University Library? Discuss their quality and utility.

Ans. A library building is a specialised structure with specific functions, so the furniture for a library has to be custom designed for each function. The needs of furniture and equipment of individual departments and sections should be given careful consideration so that the users and the staff experience ease, comfort, convenience and efficiency in their work. The kind of furniture is to be acquired is either.

(i) stock standard available from manufacturers who specialise in library furniture, or

(ii) custom-built or made to order with specification provided by the library.

The standard furniture is usually made of metal whereas the ordered furniture is made with wood. These days some firms have also started manufacturing plastic furniture for the libraries. It is advisable to visit some good libraries and some manufacturers of library furniture before deciding on the type of furniture to be ordered.

Before acquiring furniture for the library, care should be taken to:

(a) Decide the kind of furnishing suitable for a particular library.

(b) Determine what is available in the market and what can be obtained to satisfy the requirements of the library.

(c) Select and purchase furniture based on type or users, amount use, kind of material (to be stored, organised and displayed in the library) , number of staff member and future growth or changes in the library.

(d) Consultation with library staff members.

(e) Market prices, comparison of rates, etc.

Various kind of furniture are required for a library such as stack room racks, periodical display racks, catalogue card cabinet, charging desks and some special furniture items. For sitting purpose tables and chairs for the staff and the users are also required. Some of the furniture items required by a library are discussed below:

(i) Stack Room Racks

The most important piece of furniture in any library is the racks in the stack room. These are used to store books, periodicals, bound volumes of periodicals, reports, and other kinds of reading materials. Each individual rack (wooden or steel) is usually 180 cm wide, 195/225 cm high and 25/50 cm deep depending on whether it is single sided or double sided. The number of shelves in a rack is usually 5 or 6 depending on the height of the rack. A number of racks can be joined together to make one row. The popular kinds of stacks are:

— **Fixed Shelves with Double Row :** They are normal fixed shelves where material can be arranged in double rows.

— **Hinged Stacks :** Here two shelves are joined together with hinges on one side and one shelf fixed while the other is mounted in front of the hinges.

— **Rolling Stacks :** These are metal stack units mounted on ball bearing wheel placed side by side.

— **Compact Storage :** This system consists of units of three stacks, the centre row of fixed double-sided stacks at each side. This helps in increasing the capacity of the storage space.

— **Multitier Stacks :** This kind of stacking consists of stacks from floor to the roof and has become quite popular in very large libraries.

While selecting stacks for any kind of library, main consideration should be to ensure maximum space utilization, user convenience and easy movement with the stack room. There should also be adequate provision for future expansion both horizontally as well as vertically.

(ii) Periodical Display Rack

Libraries usually display periodicals for attracting the users which leads to greater use of this category of materials. Methods of display of periodicals are determined by a number of factors which include:

— Type of periodicals acquired

— Floor space available

— Layout of the library

— Types of users coming to the library

Many libraries have a separate reading room where periodicals are housed and displayed whereas in some others a general reading room accommodates all the reading materials.

For displaying periodicals, usually periodical display racks are used. These display racks are of three kinds:

— Step type

— Pigeon hole type

— Inclined type

The brief details of each type of the periodical display racks are as :

Step or Gallery type : In this type the periodicals are displayed stepwise, each step being 5 cm deep and 15 cm high. Length of the rack is generally 90 cm. There may be 4 to 5 steps and on each step 4 to 5 journals can be displayed and on a single sided rack 20-25 journals can be displayed. Double sided racks are not recommended since the unit becomes too bulky. It is better to place two single sided racks back to back if necessary. Journals are better displayed in this type, but one great disadvantage is that back issues cannot be accommodated within the unit. Normally popular magazines are displayed in this type of racks.

Pigeon hole type : This is the most popular type of display rack in libraries especially in libraries subscribing to a large number of periodicals. This type of rack has two parts, one being a cupboard in the bottom and other pigeon holes at the top. The usual height and width are 7.5 feet by 6 feet. The depth is about one foot in the pigeon hole and about 1.5 feet in the lower cupboard portion. The cupboard portion is for storing the back volumes of the periodicals and the pigeons holes hold about 36 current periodicals.

This type of display rack is very convenient and useful in the library but there is one disadvantage that the periodicals cannot be displayed properly.

Inclined type : This type of display rack is considered to be the best type and is an improvement over the earlier pigeon hole type of rack. This is a box type rack with horizontal shelves, each covered with wooden planks with an inclination to the shelf plank. The shelves can be partitioned into pigeon holes, each hole being provided with a wooden support for the periodicals. Here the inclined plank provides a better way of displaying periodicals, with the back issues in the space behind the inclined plank. Display space for 25 to 30 periodicals can be provided in one rack.

(iii) Catalogue Card Cabinets

The catalogue cabinet is the most frequently used item not only by the users but by library staff too. It is a unit of drawers full of cards specially designed to hold library cards (5" x 3") and equipped with a metal holding rods. The catalogue cabinet and its drawers are usually made of wood, metals or plastic material. These units are available in wide range of sizes starting from four drawers to about sixty drawers. For convenience and ease of use, the rows of drawers are placed on stands and the overall height of the cabinet along with the stand is usually not more than 4.5 to 5 feet that is eye level. Each tray can hold about 1,000 thick cards. Depending on the size of the library, the catalogue card cabinet can be acquired.

(iv) Charging Desk/Issue Counter

The charging desk, also called the issue counter, is the main service point of any library. It should be designed to take care of the various activities associated with the issue and return of the documents of the library. The charging desk is often specially prepared for an individual library and very seldom bought from the market. It is designed keeping in view the kind of library, available space, specific functions, and size of the library. The charging counter should have sufficient drawer space to accommodate all the issued documents records. The counter should also have sufficient shelving space for placing books which are returned by the users.

The issue counter is usually designed for two persons to work simultaneously. It is essential that sufficient leg space be provided while designing the counter. As high chairs are used by the staff working at the issue counter, a foot stool is also required. Some of the common design for the issue counter are circular, L-shaped, rectangular or U-shaped.

(v) Tables and Chairs

For use by the library staff, proper tables with suitable drawers are required. The tables to be used by the readers in the reading room are larger in size and without any drawers. The table should be atleast 29" high with blunt or round edges. Library tables are usually made of wood or metal or a combination of both.

The chairs is any library should be atleast 26" high with a knee height of 17". The chairs are required for reading hall, lounge, staff room and seminar room etc.

(vi) Other Furniture Items

In addition to the furniture items mentioned above, a few other item are required in any kind of library. These are:

(a) Display rack for newly acquired books,

(b) Book trolley for moving books from one part of the library to the other,

(c) Stands for over-sized books,

(d) Notice Board,

(e) Almirahs for storing new books,

(f) Computer tales,

(g) Foot stools for users in stack room for picking books from upper shelves,

(h) Newspaper stands with sloping top,

(i) Side racks (3-4 feet high) for keeping books, files, etc. for use by the staff, and

(j) Property counter or racks for keeping users belongings.

Library Equipments

The equipment in the library should be suitable for use by the staff and the users. The library should be provided with equipment of standard size and specifications. The kinds of equipment usually found in any library includes:

(i) Record keeping equipment

(ii) Filing cabinets

(iii) Photocopiers

(iv) Computers

(v) Miscellaneous items

(i) Record Keeping Equipments

Record - keeping equipments in the library are mainly used for keeping records of periodicals' current issues as they are received, and the back files of bound or otherwise preserved volumes. The kind of equipment to be selected for this purpose depends on the size of the library, kind of users and the number of currently received periodicals. This kind of equipment is being replaced by computerised record systems in majority of the libraries. The existing manual system is based on a unit card, one for each periodical title, on which complete details of the periodical are available. The cards are filed in transparent holders and placed in an overlapping manner with only the title portion visible. As and when new periodical issues are received, the details are noted down in appropriate columns.

Equipment used for this purpose is Kardex, Linedex or loose leaf binders which is supplied by many companies specialising in the area. Linedex is a metal cylindrical structure of 30 cm height, revolving on ball bearing, and having a knob at the top and a number of metal panels, where perforated strips of paper bearing the title of the journal subscribed by the library with their location are displayed. A simple loose leaf binder which look like bank ledgers can also be used in place of Kardex.

(ii) Filing Cabinets

Plenty of library materials needs to be filed and provision has to be made for keeping these properly. The kinds of material to filed includes - correspondence, newspaper clippings, pamphlets, patents, standards and other types of materials with odd sizes. For easy storage and fast retrieval, various types of filing equipment has been designed.

For filing of correspondence, vertical filing cabinets with drawers that can be pulled out are available. Pamphlet boxes of various kinds are available for storing pamphlets, leaf-lets, standards and patents. These boxes are available in different sizes and can open at the top of side. They are made of metal, wood or cardboard. For large drawings and designs, large steel cabinets with pull out drawers are available.

(iii) Photocopiers

For various purposes multiple copies of documents are aften needed in a library. Making multiple copies of the documents, every library needs photocopiers. Presently several companies are manufacturing photocopiers with several variation like coloured copies, size enlargement or reduction and several copies at a time. Depending on the requirements of an individual library and a availability of funds, suitable copier as per requirements can be purchased.

(iv) Computers

The library work involves lot of correspondence, maintaining records and other activities requiring typing work. Typewriters are gradually replaced by computers in most of the libraries. Computers are presently most important piece of equipment in any library as it can be used not only as a replacement of a typewriter but also for preparing automated catalogue record, serials management, maintaining records or correspondence, circulation and easy access of information. Presently, several companies in India are offering computer systems with varied configuration. Care with regard to choice of hardware, vendor and the software should be taken while selecting a computer system.

These days many libraries, which have automated their activities, are bar-coding their document. For this bar-coding reading equipment may also required.

(v) Miscellaneous Items

Besides the equipment mentioned above, some more items are required for any library which include :

— Storage cabinets (metal or wooden) for keeping office supplies,
— Stool or step ladder for reaching high shelves and roofs,
— Revolving stands,
— Vacuum cleaners,
— Air-conditioners,
— Binding equipment,
— Electric stylus for writing on spines of book,
— Microform reading equipment, and
— Non conventional indexing and filing equipments etc.

6
Library Authority and Library Committee : Role and Functions

Q. : What do you mean by library Authority? Discuss its functions.

or

Discuss the constitution of an ideal Library Authority.

or

Distinguish the Library Authority and Library Committee. Discuss the role of Librarian in this context.

or

What is library committee? Discuss its various types.

or

Library committee is not redundant authority between Librarian and head of the organization. Discuss this in the light of roles and responsibilities of library committee.

Ans. : Authority is a management concept. A manager's authority in all institution consists of the right to do such things as to make decision, assign work to do to subordinates, review the work of subordinates under recommended retention or release of subordinates on the basis of performance. Most institutional authority resides in the formal positions or officer rather than in the office holder. The purpose of authority is to perform some kind of service by means of administrative process.

Library Authority in University Libraries

University is an authonomous body. For the Central Universities,

President of India is the Chancellor and for State Universities, the Governor of the concerned States.

Types of University Authority

The University authority is devided into two types. These are:

Central University Authority : The President or Vice-president of India and Senate - Syndicate, Vice-chancellor are the Executive Authorities of Central University.

Library Committee, the Deans of faculties and the University Librarian are the staff agency.

The Deputy Librarian, the Assistant librarian are the Line Agency.

State University Authority : The Governor of the particular State (Chancellor), Pro-Chancellor, Senate, Syndicate, and the Vice - Chancellor of the concern University are the Executive Authority.

Library Committee and University Librarian are the staff Authority.

The Deputy Librarian and the Assistant librarian are the line agency. In University, the Administrative Board (Syndicate or Executive Council) provides the library committee to assist the libraries in the allocation of book funds and in the formulation of board, general policy of library development.

Powers and Functions of Library Authority

The following are the powers of authority.

(i) It has an administrative process, to implement the functions and fulfil the objective.

(ii) Administrative process is tested with certain powers.

(iii) To test certain power to carry on certain functions.

(iv) Authority should have status. Both are inseparable.

As for as its functions are concerned, a library authority contributes in :

— Policy making,

— Supervising, and

— Non - Supervising Decisions.

Library Authority vs. Library Committee

The word 'authority' implies a person having power to do something whereas 'committee' means a body consisting of certain persons which are assigned a particular job. Such committees mostly supervise and advice the Librarians in matters in which public participation are essential. 'Committee' is a representative body of the people. The committee may be elected or nominated by the people themselves. It comprises a group of persons drawn from within the library and experts from outside, including representatives from the user community.

Library Committee

The library committee means of body consisting of certain persons, which is assigned a particular job. Such committees mostly supervise and advice the libraries in matters in which public participation is essential.

Need, Purpose and Role of library Committees

The need for library committees is felt and recognized for the following reasons.

(i) As libraries is not revenue earning institutions, therefore all are supported by the public exchequer. Committees built into the structure of library management, comprising experts, users and others from outside the library, give a public image that the library is run not merely by bureaucratic authority and power but by a democratic process.

(ii) Committees perform useful functions in providing management an authority and strength to implement policies, plans and programmes with confidence and commitment.

(iii) As committees usually have experts with experience from outside the library hence dispassionate views and advice can be obtained on crucial and critical issues thus steering the library through difficult periods.

(iv) Operating through committees helps the management to delegate and decentralise responsibilities and duties and thus gives a collective authority to decisions.

The main purposes of library committee are :

(i) To give the management collective advice and guidance or views on matters connected with the development of the library, approve plans, polices, programmes and oversee their proper execution and implementation.

(ii) They may also be entrusted with the task of evaluation of the performance and progress of the library to give it direction for future development.

(iii) These committees do not have executive powers or authority to involve or interfere in the day to day management of the library.

(iv) The committee acts as a buffer and an interpreter of the needs of the people.

(v) The library committee assesses the financial needs of the library in accordance with the national library standards.

(vi) The committees can appoint the Librarian who is competent. It can also make an instrument in the hands of Librarian as if can quite cleverly cultivate the ideas in the committee's minds, which he wants.

The role of library committees should be positive and forward-looking. It should not take any partisan view of any matter brought before it but take an objective stand on all matters vital to the growth and development of the library. Temptations of members of the committee to interfere with the working of the library will seriously jeopardize the library's future.

Kinds of Library Committee

A library may have a numbers of committees depending upon its size, the nature of activities and operations. However, committees are usually constituted according to statutory requirements. Generally, the following kinds of library committees are in practice :-

1. Executive Committee,
2. Adhoc Committee,
3. Nominated Committee,
4. Reporting Committee,
5. Recommending Committee,
6. Self Perpetuating Committee, and
7. Sub - Committee.

1. Executive Committee : It is a committee with delegated powers by the authority. This committee can be said the most powerful committee. The local authority cannot interfere in its work and it also need not to report its decisions to the library authority.

2. Adhoc Committee : It is the special committee for the supervision and control of libraries' functioning. It is speedy in its decisions and it can accommodate coopted members of performing a specific job. The Madras Public Libraries Act, 1948 provides for the appointment of such committee. This committee is more or less independent and it has nothing to do with the Local Government Bodies. This committee is also called statutory authority committee. It has the advantage of being independent of politics. It takes the decision very fastly. But sometimes it comes into clash with the Local Government Bodies specially in the matter of collection of taxes.

3. Nominated Committee : Nominated or elected committee is constituted by a larger committee or the authority to look after the works and matters of the library. Certain functions are delegated to such a committee. The provision of such type committee was made for the first time in the Andhra Pradesh Public Libraries, Act, 1960 under chapter II. It is an effective committee.

4. Reporting Committee : It is an effective and powerful committee who has got powers to decide the policies within certain limits. Its decisions and action taken are simple and are reported to the authority only for the information. It does not require the confirmation from the supreme authority. It is co-operating and helpful to the Librarian.

5. Recommending Committee : This type of committee has no powers but it can recommend certain proposals for governing the library which are subject to the approval of the library authority. It is very slow in character. This type of committee is found only in England.

6. Self-Prepetuating Committee : It is created and exists in case of libraries operating under special character of statutes. Such committee has sole authority and is independent as regard the control and management of libraries under it. It need not to report its activities to the higher authority. In USA and South Africa, we found the example of such committee.

7. Sub-Committee : In addition to the above committees, the authority may appoint sub - committee according to the needs. The library committee also appoints a sub - committee in order to look after the functions like maintenance of accounts, purchase of books, physical verification and other such important matters.

Delegation of Powers

In case of Executive/Reporting Committee the real powers are delegated by the library authorities to such Library Committees which are free to take decisions within the framework of the broad policy. The library authorities generally delegate all the powers to the library authority except the following :

1. Raising of loan,
2. Levying of rate/tax,
3. Raising the rate limit,
4. Concluding agreements with other agencies to combine the service units in order to effect economy and to avoid wastage of energies,
5. Deciding the appointment, suspension and dismissal of senior officials of the library,
6. Sanctioning new library plans,
7. Sanctioning expenditure for new buildings, and
8. Sanctioning new library service units.

Powers and Functions of the Library Committee

The powers and functions vary according to the nature of the committee. In case of Recommending Committee these will be too less, but in case of executive committee will be increased. The Librarian puts all proposals for discussion at the Library Committee meetings. These functions relate broadly to the following items : -

1. Library Building : Library Committee should ensure that the building is functional and modular if proper services are to be provided to the readers. The building would be centrally located natural light and air must be provided in the proper manner. Necessary arrangement should be made for the proper maintenance of the library.

2. Library Furniture and Fittings : Adequate, proper and cozy library furniture should be provided so that the readers stay comfortable. Only standard furniture articles should be provided, so that any number of articles identical in nature can be added in future.

3. Library Staff : Library Committee should employ qualified and adequate staff for the library, so that standard library services are provided to the readers. The library committee should accept norms for fixing the number of staff members and their salary scales with sufficient opportunities for promotion so that the staff member could stay there for a fairly long time.

4. Library Finance and Book Collection : A library committee should provide enough funds for purchasing the basic book-collection and for adding latest books in a library. A proper committee should be set for the book selection, so that lists of books are thoroughly scrutinized to avoid the purchase of undesirable books.

5. Library Rules : A set of rules should be framed for the readers but they should not be too rigid but are flexible and suit the needs of the readers. No monetary obligations should be put on the readers.

6. Library Accounts and Audit : The committee should provide a proper machinery for checking the library accounts. It may appoint an account sub - committee for auditing accounts.

7. Library Acts and Rules : The committee should keep all the acts and rules up-to-date. Necessary amendments should be made from time to time.

8. Library Cooperation : The library committee should try to get cooperation amongst the various branches of the library within a locality.

9. Standard Library Service : The committee should try to provide best library services in all the localities under its jurisdiction by opening new branches with adequate numbers of staff-members and providing all the services as far as possible.

10. Library Policies : The committee should lay down the policy for the day to day work and guidelines to help the Librarian to work effeciently.

Advantages of Library Committee

1. It helps the librarian in carrying out the administration of library more efficiently.
2. It serves both as co-ordinating and policy making body.
3. It adds to the prestige of the library.
4. The Librarian with the help of committee members can get the important and complicated works done in a easy way.

5. The administration needs support and this is possible by the Committee.
6. The committee members may assess the financial needs of the library and finally they may arrange for more and more funds.
7. It ensures better understanding between the management and the readers.
8. It can convince the government and the people about the needs of the library service for the well being of the community.
9. It can explore and use modern methods for broadening the library resources and facilities.

Disadvanatges of Library Committee

1. Sometimes the library committee may take hasty decision resulting in the lowering of prestige of the library authority.
2. Impartial decisions cannot be taken at many times as interested parties can influence the library committee.
3. The library committee may be overwhelmed by the local feelings and larger interest may be sacrified.
4. Sometimes an area may lack really capable people and inefficiency may be the result.

Librarian and the Library Committee

The committee should meet either monthly or after longer intervals as the case may be. To conduct a meeting there must be some presiding officer. A Chairman to be elected by its members provided there is no ex-officio Chairman. Vice - Chairman may also be elected to preside over the meetings in the absence of the chairman. Librarian generally serves as the Secretary of the Committee.

The Librarian should always discuss the agenda with the chairman before it is issued to the members. While sending an agenda for a committee meeting, care should be taken to supply the members all the requests information about the items on the agenda so that the decisions are arrived at expediously and properly. The agenda should be accompanied with a forwarding letter in which the members are informed regarding the time, date and venue of the next meeting of the committee.

The agenda should provide for the following items :

(i) **Minutes of the last Meetings :** The decisions taken by the committee in the last meeting are to be presented in the next meeting for having formal approval of the committee.

(ii) **List of Books for Approval :** The Librarian should submit a list of books to be purchased for the library. If there is a sub - committee on Book Selection, Librarian to get approval and presents a report to the library committee.

(iii) **Purchase of Stationary and Other Equipments :** The Librarian submits a detailed list of requirements for the next year along with comparative statement of rates of the items if they are costly.

(iv) Bills for various articles purchased.

(v) Estimates of heavy plans of alterations in the building.

(vi) **Raising of funds :** Librarian should provide true picture of the financial position.

(vii) Estimates for the provision of additional services and staff or opening of new branches.

Lastly, the Librarian should submit a monthly report to the committee about the working of the library during the previous month. This report consists of staff and services.

The Chairman of the committee must be fully briefed by the librarian in all matters likely to arise from minutes of the last meeting and from the current agenda. The Librarian should take note of the deliberations and decisions in the meeting and at the end a draft of the minutes be prepared. The minutes of the meeting should be brief as well as clear.

7

Annual Report, Library Rules, Library Statistics and Library Publicity & Display

Q. : What are the purposes of Annual Report? Which items of information should be included in it and how can these be presented effectively?

Ans. It is a prevalent practice in administration that the operating units should submit the details of their activities to the central office. These details of activities are known as reports. Such reports may be periodic - weekly, fortnightly, monthly, quarterly, half yearly or annual.

An annual report of library is the survey of work carried out during the preceding year. An annual report summarizes activities and achievements of the library. It is a type of reporting by the Librarian to the higher authorities.

Need of Annual Reports

A library is expected to report about its working to the higher authorities (Library committee or Board of Trustees or Head of Parent body) periodically to keep them informed about its achievements, shortcomings, problems and suggestions for improvement. "According to ordinance of University of Delhi, the Librarian shall address a written report to the Vice-Chancellor each year summarising the activities and achievements of the library under his management." An annual report is expected by the Vice - Chancellor because it would like to have justification for spending on the University library. Similarly a public library would have to justify its cost of the public. A special library would have to give justification for the money spent to its parent organization.

Functions of Annual Reports

An annual report performs the following functions : -

(i) It keeps the authorities well informed about activities and achievements of the library.

(ii) It serves as a publicity media towards attracting the users.

(iii) Comparison of annual reports of different years make enable the librarian to determine strong and weak points of the library. This will help him to improve the library.

(iv) Comparison of annual report with standard for staff, finance, collection etc. will enable the Librarian to put forward a case for additional staff, finance, etc.

Objectives of Annual Reports

1. Intimation to Managing Committee

The annual reports are the best medium to make known about the working of library services to the members of managing committee. With the help of annual reports, one can know all the information regarding library and its various services at one place.

2. Library Publicity

The annual reports are also one of the media of library publicity. All the details regarding purchase of books, way of providing library services to its readers, information about technical service of the library, all can be best understood with the help of annual repots.

3. Helpful in Urgent Needs

As all essential information are available at one place in reports, one can draw the attention of higher authorities, with the help of annual reports about the needs of the library sincerely.

4. Evaluation of Financial Position

One can also evaluate the position of finance through the statistics of budget in annual reports. If the finance of library are not good enough, that can be arranged going through the comparative study of the different items of the budget appeared in annual reports.

5. Evaluation of Job

One can also know the status of different workers working in different sections of the library and can judge their performance. If a particular department is not working properly or up to the mark, the efforts can be made to enhance its working by going through the annual reports.

6. Useful for Researchers

The annual reports are also useful source of information for the researchers.

Contents of Annual Report

An annual report may be published in two parts. Part I may consist of descriptive part and Part II may give statistical data.

The following heads may be included in Part I:

General review : It should form introduction, summarizing the significant features of activities and achievements during the year as well as the important developments planned for the next year. It should also describe the problems and give suggestions towards the solution.

Users

Collection

Classification and cataloguing

Services to users

Circulation

Reference service

Indexing and abstracting services

Newspaper clippings

Reprography

Library extension service

Maintenance

Finance

- Expenditure
- Income

Staff

Building and equipment

Publication programme

Miscellaneous

Part II will contain statistical data in the form of tables.

Draft of Annual Report

Year ....

(A) General

1. Name of the Library ....
2. Nature of Library ....
3. Year of Establishment ....
4. Rural / Urban ....
5. Working hours ....
6. No. of Days of Holidays in a Year ....

(B) Clientele

1. Total Number of Members ....
2. Male ....
3. Female ....
4. Children ....
5. Number of Members enrolled in Current Year ....
6. Ratio of Memberships ....

(C) Book Stock

		Books	Periodicals
1.	Number of Books at the starting of Current Year	....	....
2.	Number of Books purchased in Current Year	....	....
3.	Number of Books withdrawal in Current Year	....	....
4.	Number of Books at the end of the Current Year	....	....

(D) Technical Service

1. Whether the Books are Classified or Not ....
2. Name of Classification Scheme Used ....

3. Name of Cataloguing Code Used ....
4. Physical Form of Catalogue ....

(E) Staff

1. Total Number of Library Staff ....
2. Professional ....
3. Semi-professional ....
4. Non - professional ....

(F) Circulation Section

1. Issue System Used ....
2. Total Number of Books issued in the Year ....
3. Average Number of Books issued per Day ....
4. Number of Books issued Subject - wise ....

(G) Reference Section

1. Number of Reference Books ....
2. Number of Books Used per Day ....
3. Number of Reference Queries per Day ....
4. Number of Readers used the Section per Day ....

(H) Indexing, Abstracting and Documentation

1. Number of Index Made ....
2. Number of Index Used by the Readers ....
3. Number of Article Abstracted ....
4. Number of Article Abstracted Used by the Readers ....

(I) Mobile Library Service

1. Number of Village ....
2. Average of Works per Week ....
3. Number of Books Issued/Returned ....

(J) Finance

(a) Expenditure

i. Recurring ....

ii. Non-Recurring ....

iii. Total ....

(b) Revenue

(K) Cost Accounting

(L) Miscellaneous

Date ....

Signature of Librarian

Q. : Clarify the significance of Library Statistics. Give the structure of different types of statistical tables maintained by a University Library.

Ans. : The terms 'statistics' is derived from the Latin word 'Status' which means a political state. In ancient days, facts and figures were required by the kings for their administration particualarly related to foodstuff, finance and man-power available in their states. Therefore in the past statistics was known as the 'Science of Kings', or the "Science of Statecraft." But its scope now a days has extended tremendously. It covers all problems related to the mankind. Thus, this science is very much different from what it was in earlier days.

Now-a-days, "Statistics may be defined as the collection presentation, analysis and enterpretation of numerical data".

In libraries, the statistics can be used in measuring the progress or regress within a given time if the comparative figures of past and present are given. It helps the administration in getting the clear picture of the various activities of the library.

The tabulated figures of income and expenditures in various heads of the previous may be best utilized in reshaping the future plan and current annual budget of the library. They are useful for the members of the Library Committee in knowing the achievements and demands made by the public. The demand may relate to reader's choice and curiosities of books, periodicals, extension services, information and reprographic services, bibliographical services and documentation services etc. Thus, statistics serves in many ways for library development. It also indicates the strength or weakness of a particular section or sections of the library. On the basis of these figures authority can justify in demanding more books, more staff, more fund, more space and more furniture to cope with the increased demand. Statistics is also used as a means of publicity to make the library more popular in the community or elsewhere. Therefore, it should be compiled carefully and in a simple self explanatory form. Moreover, the statistics are the most appropriate basis for preparation of annual reports too.

Usefulness of statistics

Management would like to know 'how well the library is doing?' Comparison of statistics over a few years can indicate the position of the library. Librarian can use statistics for the following purposes:

— To compile an annual report.

— To measure efficiency of different sections or individuals.

— For planning of a library and its services. On the basis of statistics, a new service can be planned or an existing service can be improved. Statistics will indicate, whether there is likely to be enough demand for the new service.

— To prepare a case for increase in funds and staff.

— To present to users and management, the achivements of the library.

Kinds of Statistics

The kinds of statistics to be maintained may vary from library to library. This will depend upon the use to be made of statistics.

Statistics may be collected about the following :

Acquisition

Classification

Cataloguing

Membership

Issue of books

Reference service

Periodicals

Others

The basic statistics, which should be collected are described below:

Acquisition : Number of documents obtained by purchase, gift, exchange and membership. This may be analysed by type of documents and by subject.

Classification : Number of different types of documents classified. This may be analysed by type of documents, by individual classifier and by subject.

Cataloguing : Number of documents catalogued and number of cards prepared. This may be analysed by individual cataloguer and type of documents.

Membership : Number of members by category and the Number of members who visited the library.

Issue : Number of books and other documents issued. Issue statistics may be gathered language-wise, user-wise, category of document-wise and subject-wise etc.

Reference Service : Number of queries in terms of ready and long range reference service. Number of queries which could not be answered. Number of entries included in bibliographies, indexing and abstracting services.

Periodicals : Statistics regarding periodicals may be maintained separately. This may include statistics based on frequency of publication.

Others : Other statistics may include figures about expenditure on staff, collection, equipment, etc. and the figures about staff of different categories.

Limitations

Statistics have certain limitations. The limitations are given below:

— Statistics are quantitative in nature. As a result, these do not reveal the quality of work carried out.

— Statistics do not reveal the entire story of a library.

— Statistics are true on average only.

Collection

Diaries maintained by different sections can be highly useful. Daily/ weekly/monthly/quarterly statistical reports sent by different sections to the Chief Librarian are considered useful sources of statistics. For statistical returns, routing forms should be designed. The forms should be designed very carefully and should be periodically revised in the light of experience. The specimen form for some of them are as follows:

DAILY STATISTICS REGISTER : CIRCULATION

Sl. No.	*Section Category*		*Date* *1 2 3 4 5 6 7 8...31*	*Total*
1.	Reference	L R		
2.	Philosophy	L R		
3.	Religion	L R		
4.	Social Sciences	L R		
5.	Language	L R		
6.	Pure Sciences	L R		
7.	Appl. Sciences	L R		
8.	Art	L R		

9.	Literature	L / R
10.	History	L / R
11.	Visitors Attendance	
12.	Librarian's Signature	

Abbreviations : L.- Lending
R.- Reading

This register be kept uptodate by making entries in each column daily. This gives a clear picture of books issued for reading room and home lending. The total number of books issued be counted daily, monthly and yearly. This is also useful in knowing the reading habit and choice of readers.

STATISTICS OF PERIODICALS

Subject	*Daily*		*Weekly*		*Fortnightly*		*Monthly*		*Qly.*		*H.Y.*		*Y.*	
Lang.	*S*	*C*	*S*	*C*	*S*	*C*	*S*	*C*	*S*	*C*	*S*	*C*	*S*	*C*
Hindi														
Bengali														
English (Indian)														
English (Foreign)														
Misc.														
Total														

Abbreviations : S.-Subscribed
C.-Complimentary.

In the above form the Number of Daily, Weekly, Fortnightly, Monthly, Quarterly, Half Yearly, and Yearly periodicals received be filled up in each column and at last the total number be counted. This chart gives a clear picture of magazines received in the library during the year.

STATISTICS OF BOOKS ISSUED

Subject	*Lending*	*Year*	
		Reading	*Total*
1. Reference			
2. Philosophy			
3. Religion			
4. Social Sciences			
5. Language			
6. Pure Sciences			
7. Applied Sciences			
8. Literature - Fiction / Non-fiction			
9. History			
10. Travel			
11. Biography			
Total			
Hindi and other Subjects			
1. Hindi-Fiction / Non-Fiction			
2. Bengali			
3. Sanskrit			
4. Urdu			
5. Children Section			
Total			

By the above statistics, one can have an idea of the subjects and languages which are popular among the readers.

STATISTICS : VOLUMES ADDED LANGUAGEWISE

Language	*2001-02*	*2002-03*	*2003-04*
1. English			
2. Hindi			
3. Sanskrit			
4. Bengali			
5. Urdu			
6. Others			
Total			

This statistics presents a clear and comparative figures of books added languagewise to the library during the particular year.

STATISTICS : TOTAL NUMBER OF VOLUMES

Languages	*2001-02*	*2002-03*	*2003-04*
I. General			
1. English			
2. Hindi			
3. Sanskrit			
4. Bengali			
5. Urdu			
6. Others			
II. Govt. Publications			
III. Bound volumes of Magazines			
IV. Miscellaneous			
Total			

STATISTICS OF BOOKS RECEIVED

Year...............

1.	By Purchase	(a) Books	Generallia	Phil.	Rel.
		(b) G.P.			
		(c) Misc.			
		Total			
2.	By Exchange	(a) Books			
		(b) G.P.			
		(c) Misc.			
		Total			
3.	By Gift	(a) Books			
		(b) G.P.			
		(c) Misc.			
4.	By Other Source	(a) Books			
		(b) G.P.			
		(c) Misc.			
	Grand Total				

The above statistics maintained by the acquisition section will be able to give the information about various materials acquired by the library in different subjects.

STATISTICS OF CLASSIFICATION WORK

Sl. No.	*Employees Name and Designation*	*No. of books Classified Datewise*	*Total*	*Remarks*
		1 2 3 4 5 6 ... 31		

In order to know the output of whether the persons on duty are discharging their duties fully satisfactorily or not, it is essential to maintain the statistics daily.

Similar to the classification section the statistics should be maintained for the work performed in the cataloguing section.

Visitor's attending to the Library belong to various occupations, age, sex and places. They come to the library for different purposes like – study, research reference or simply to have a glance of the Library. A visitor's register is kept on the entrance door of the Library where they are required to fill up the columns with their signature. This register may contain the following columns :

STATISTICS OF DAILY VISITORS

Date	*Sl. No.*	*Name of the visitors and Address*	*Occupation Age*	*Sex*	*Purpose*	*Remarks*

To study the groups of readers and visitors, it is essential to have the information in the above proforma. This may help while the books and other reading materials for purchase.

In the administrative section the figures of income and expenditure should also be maintained.

Year..... ......

Income			*Expenditure*		
(a) By Govt. grants	Rs.	Paise	(a) By Establishment	Rs.	Paise
(b) By own source			(b) By purchase of books		
(c) By donation and other sources			(c) By purchase of Furniture		
			(d) By cost of binding		
			(e) By subscription of journals		
			(f) By contingencies		
			(g) Others		
Total			Total		

Earlier, the statistics were not considered necessary and there was no confirmity in compiling the figures. But now the statistics has become a necessary part of any report to be submitted by the Library. The facts of the report supplemented by the figures or statistics carries more weight and become more convincing.

Q. : Write notes on the followings:

1. Library Rules

2. Library Publicity and Displays

Ans.

1. LIBRARY RULES

Libraries being social institutions, their managements have a special responsibility to see that the use of their resources, facilities and services are regulated properly so that there is no room for misuse, discrimination or scope for obtaining any special favours to an individual or group. It is therefore, a general practice, for libraries, to lay down rules and regulations in the use of the library, applicable equally to all categories of users, without any discrimination.

Purposes of Library Rules

The purposes behind framing the rules are :

(i) to enable the users to get the maximum out of the library resources including books, furniture, equipment, building, etc. For instance, a library may allow borrowing of maximum number of volumes for a maximum duration but a book in great demand, may be kept in reserve section and issued for a short duration, say two hours or so;

(ii) to prevent the misuse of library resources;

(iii) to avoid too strict or troublesome which may be required to curb a few dishonest persons in the community;

(iv) to allow the discretion to the librarian to take a decision on his own as a special case to allow a special privilege, (e.g. to issue a reference book, to issue reference book, to issue a book to a person, who does not have a reader's ticket, to reissue a book, etc.).

Users of the library should regard the rigid enforcement of the rules as an aid rather than a hindrance in the use of the library. The rules are be framed for increasing the use of the library rather than curbing its use.

Factors for Framing Rules

In framing rules, one should take into consideration the following factors:

(1) Number and kinds of users and their requirements. Special rules would have to be formulated for teachers, scholars and student. It the number of readers is small, it may be possible to liberalize the conditions of loan.

(2) Kind of materials as certain material cannot be issued out e.g. reference materials, theses and rare books. Very often the rule is that users must use the rare books and theses in the presence of the staff.

(3) Kind of library, for e.g., in a special library attached to a research origanization the rules should be liberal.

(4) Facilities: Number of seats (if seats are less, then provide more books for lending).

(5) Kinds of services to be rendered (e.g., Reservation, reprography, inter-library loan, bibliographical services etc.).

(6) Kind of philosophy of librarianship acceptable by the users.

Scope of the Rules

Main points or factors to be covered in the library rules are :

(a) Hours of opening,

(b) Holidays,

(c) Information regarding membership (who can enrol as a member),

(d) Admission to the library (who shall be admitted. Do's and don'ts to be observed inside the library).

(e) Loan privilege:

  (i) Number of reader's tickets and

  (ii) Loss of tickets.

(f) Conditions of loan (How may volumes of different categories, a members can borrow, publications which cannot be borrowed, period of loan, amount of fine, conditions for renewal of loan).

(g) General (A Librarian may be given discretion to refuse under special circumstances, admission into library to any person or use of any book without assigning any reason thereof. In case of an infringement of rules, a Librarian should have the power to withdraw the privilege of admission to and of borrowing books from the library).

Model Library Rules

While the general purpose of library rules and regulations remain very much the same in all types of libraries; their contents and the details are bound to vary according to the kinds of users they serve and the nature of services they offer.

The following is a set of model library rules governing circulation work and a few other matters connected with the use of a public library:

Name of the Library :

Address:

Telephone :	*Telex:*
E-mail :	

1.	Hours of opening		The hours, when the... library will be open to the public, shall be fixed by the Library Committee from time to time. The Library Committee has decided as follows for the time being. The library shall be open to the public on all days from 8 a.m. to 9 p.m. **Note:** The loan counter shall be closed half an hour before the closing of the library.
2.	Admission to the Library	21	No person, who is not of sound mind, nor clean in person, nor properly dressed, shall be admitted into the library. **Note:** The decision of the Librarian, or his deputy during his absence, in regard to these matters shall be final. The Rules may provide for admission by special permit in the cas of specified classes of persons.
		22	Person desirous of using the library shall enter his name and address

			legibly in the gate register kept for the purpose, such entry shall be taken as an acknowledgement that the person agrees to conform to the rules of the library.
		221	Sticks, umbrellas, boxes and other receptacles and such other articles as are prohibited by the circulation staff shall be left at the entrance at the property counter.
		222	Dogs and other animals shall not be admitted.
3.	Conduct with in Library	31	Silence shall be strictly observed in the library.
		32.	Spitting and smoking are strictly prohibited.
		33	Sleeping is strictly prohibited.
		34	Switch off mobile inside the library.
		35	No person shall write upon, damage, or make any mark upon any book, manuscript or map, belonging to the library.
		36	No tracing or mechanical reproduction shall be made without the express permission from the librarian.
		37	A person shall be responsible for any damage done by him to the books or other property of the library. He will be required to replace such books or other property damaged or pay the value thereof. If one book of a set is damaged, the whole set shall be liable to be replaced.
		38	Before leaving the library each person shall return to the circulation

staff any books, manuscripts or maps taken by him for consultation.

39 Cases of incivility on the part of library staff, or other failure in the service, should be reported immediately to the Librarian or his deputy during his absence.

4. Loan privileges

41 **Membership:** In a public library any of the following is entitled to take out books on loan on enrollment as a member of the library:

(i) Any person living within the area of the library and guaranteed by another known resident within the area of the library

(ii) Any person employed in an institution within the area of the library and guaranteed by the head of the institution.

42 **Enrollment:** To get enrolled as a member, a person shallfill up and sign a Form of Enrollment, which can be had free of cost at the library counter (and make a deposit of ...)

Note : The portion of the above rule shown in brackets varies from library to library. Some libraries prefer to omit this clause.

43 **Reader's Ticket:** Each member shall be given as many reader's tickets as the number of volumes, he/ she is entitled to have with him/her on loan at one time.

431 The tickets of a member will be valid for twelve months. They can be renewed by filling up a fresh Form

of Enrollment and returning to the Librarian all the expired tickets along with it.

432 A book will be lent to a member only in exchange of the tickets. This will be handed back to the member when the person returns the book, unless it is returned after due date, in which case the ticket will be handed back only after overdue charge is paid.

433 A week's notice shall be given before a deposit is withdrawn. No deposit shall be repaid until all the books outstanding against the member and all his member's tickets have been duly returned and all the dues from the person are paid.

Note: Rule 433 will be deleted if the portion of Rule 42 shown in brackets is deleted.

44 **Loss of Tickets:** A member who has lost a ticket shall make a written report of the same to the Librarian.

441 Three months' time shall elapse (or any stipulated period) after the date of such notice, before a duplicate ticket can be issued. During this period, the member shall attempt to trace and recover the ticket if possible and send a second report at the end of the period, stating the result of his endeavours.

442 If the ticket has not been traced, the member shall give an indemnity bond in the prescribed form and pay a fee... for each duplicate ticket required.

443 After the receipt of the indemnity bond and the fee, the duplicate ticket will be issued.

444 If a member, who has lost one or more tickets, applied for withdrawal of deposit amount, no action will be taken on such application till the expiry of six months after the report of loss of tickets. If the ticket is not recovered by the member before the end of that period, the member shall give indemnity bond in the prescribed from in respect of the lost tickets. After the receipt of the indemnity bond, the application for withdrawal will be dealt with in the usual way.

Note: This rule will be deleted if the portion of Rule 42 shown in brackets is deleted.

5. Conditions of Loan

51 Each member may borrow on loan not more than ... separate volumes at one time. The person must make his own arrangement for the conveyance of books to and from the library or any of the delivery stations, except that in the case of handicapped members, books may be delivered once a week at their residence on payment of an advance quarterly subscription of...

52 Before leaving the counter, the member shall satisfy as to whether the book lent is in sound physical condition; and if not, the member shall immediately bring the matter to the notice of the Librarian or his deputy in his absence otherwise the

member is liable to be held responsible for the replacement of the book by a sound copy.

53 If one book of a set is damaged or lost, the member concerned shall be liable to replace the whole set.

54 Periodical publications, directories, works difficult to replace, and such other works, as may be declared reference books by the Librarian, shall not be lent out.

55 Members are not allowed to sub-lend the books of the library.

56 All books on loan shall be returned on expiry of stipulated period from the date of issue.

57 Books temporarily in special demand may be lent for such shorter period as may be necessary or may be temporarily declared reference books under Rule 55.

58 Loans may at any time be terminated by order of the Librarian.

59 If a book is not returned to the library when due, an overdue charge of ... per volume per day shall be levied.

591 Loan may be renewed for a further period, provided:

(i) The renewal application reaches the Librarian not less than three and not more than five clear days before the date on which the book is due;

(ii) No other reader has applied for the book in the meantime; and

(iii) Not more than three consecutive renewals shall be

			allowed for the same book without its production to the library for inspection.
			In case of condition (ii) is not satisfied, the Librarian shall sent a letter to the member concerned and the book shall be returnable on the due date.
		592	A member against who any overdue or other charge is outstanding shall not be allowed to borrow books (or withdraw the deposit) until the person has paid the amount due.
6.	General	60	The Librarian may refuse, under special circumstances, admission into the library to any person or the use of any book without assigning any reason thereof.
		61	The Library Committee may refuse, under special circumstances any application for the privilege of loan of books without assigning any reason thereof.
		62	The Library Committee may grant special loans on such conditions as it may prescribe.
		63	Any infringement o the rules will render the privilege of admission to and of borrowing books from the library liable to forfeiture.

Concluding, it can be said that the rules to be framed by a library should be worked in such a way that an average user can understand these. The main rules should be printed on the library tickets, book label, pocket and back cover of the book. The rules should be formulated carefully keeping in view the different factors considered in relation to the type of users, resources and philosophy of the Librarian.

2. LIBRARY PUBLICITY AND DISPLAY

The library is a social institution designed to serve the people with knowledge that will enable them to exercise and to continue exercising there sovereignty. It is a function of the library to serve the democracy so that democracy may function effectively and may survive. To make public/readers aware of library services and make a library famous, various measures are taken introducing them to the resources, facilities and services of the library, which constitute library display, brochures and sign boards etc. With the help of these displays, a user find himself very convenient in using the library.

1. Sign Boards

To facilitate the readers to find their desired materials from the ocean of books, charts showing the general arrangement and location of books should be kept at the entrance of the stockroom. Every row of racks at both ends should be provided with signboards to indicate subjects contained therein. Besides this, each shelf should hold shelf lables. The use of library rests entirely on the methods of work and the nature of service rendered in it.

2. Library Brochure

In modern libraries, as a part of their users' service or user education programmes, well designed brochures describing the major functions and activities of the library, are prepared and produced to be distributed to all the users of the library. These library brochures are attarctively printed with coloured photographs and pictures, maps and other illustrations to guide users in the use of resources, facilities and services of the library. Such brochures may contain :

— a topographical plan of the library indicating its various units, in particular, its service units such as reading rooms, open stacks, periodical display and reading room, reference room and reference counter, circulation counter, the public catalogue/ research cubicles, reprographic unit, audio-visual room, if any etc.;

— description of the document collection of the library with its subject ramification, their organisation and location;

— details of library, bibliographical, documentation and information services the library offers;

— facilities for photocopying, special reading rooms for microforms;

— the publications of the library: its current accessions, indexing and abstracting bulletins; special bibliographies, etc.;

— names of senior officers of the library who will be available for assistance and help or consultation or service, including the head of the library;

— any other special feature of the library which the user should know;

— extracts of important rules and regulations such as library hours, list of holidays, registration of members, borrowing and reference facilities etc. and the

— price list of publications and services.

3. Display

The purpose of libraries is to give the maximum service to the maximum public and for this publicity arrangements are necessary for efficient service and easy use of library resources. Advertising mediums include newspapers and other local publications, book lists and bulletin published by the library leaflets, circular, letters, monthly lists and poster notice of new books, bulletin boards, display racks, printed and handwritten poster, exhibition, window displays, visits by groups to the library weeks and so on. For free use of library resources following things are also essential :

(i) Attractive and comfortable building in a good location,

(ii) An efficient administration and courteous treatment to readers from the Librarian and the staff. The attractiveness of building will induce the public to visit the library; and when he is in the building the Librarian and the staff will impress upon their minds, the necessity of taking advantage of the facilities offered there.

(iii) Information regarding the working of the library i.e., the rules for use of books be properly displayed at the prominent place in the library.

The list of holidays and working hours be also circulated amongst the readers. Any change of working hours should be notified in time and exhibited inside the building as well as outside. Members of the library be informed what facilities are available at any hour of any particular day. The hour of opening should be printed on all guide books and pasted on all notice boards. It is also essential that the Librarian should move freely in the public and arrange lectures and library matters which will create very favourable atmosphere for use of libraries. The display of books jackets in the library is one of the most popular forms of publicity. If possible such display may be arranged outside the library campus also at the important places of the area. This should be always kept in mind that jackets are changed regularly.

Display of books also catches the attention of readers and create interest for reading. It is possible to reserve the 'Book Display Racks' for new books. Such racks should be pointed in bold letters as *"Books of Today", "Recent Additions", "Latest Arrivals"* etc. The kind of display gives fruitful result. The Call No. and Accession No. should also be mentioned clearly on the jackets so that the readers may get them easily when they are mixed in the stacks.

4. Library Directory

The Library Directory should explain the details of its resources and the way to make the fullest use of them. A well written Directory will prove of great services to the readers who hesitate to approach the staff for personal help.

5. Library Lectures

The book talks or library lectures may also be organized at frequent intervals suited for every group of readers. The lectures are not intended simply for the amusement but for imparting solid information. The lecturer should recommend books on the subject matter of the lecture. Such books available in the library be kept open for those who will like to consult them. This lecture methods will create the reading interest among readers and thus the number of readers will increase.

6. Guide to Classification & Cataloguing

In order to give full benefit to the readers for use of library resources it requires number of guides about the form of classification adopted in the library. Although scientific scheme of classification is logical and planned to suit the readers requirement but the same is not self explanatory. The readers may be bewildered and confused with the system in use although the same may be of much use to them. In the Library Hand-book or Directory a chapter may be included to the scheme of classification and its use. A detail chart showing the subject and its number be placed on the entrance, of every stacks and near the card catalogue cabinet. The subject label above the Book-Cases should include the classification numbers.

Similarly, the Library Catalogue requires considerable explanation in brief and annotated form and also the assistance of the staff. The Library Directory may also devote one chapter on the explanation of catalogue for its use. Such explanation should include the following items:

(i) Methods of finding books by author, title or subject,

(ii) Rules of alphabetization,

(iii) The name of Code adopted.

The guide should be printed in leaflet form and be circulated among the readers. The card cabinet of the catalogue should be well guided clearly. The letter guides are essential inside the cabinet also for its easy use. This procedure can save the time of the reader and staff as well.

7. Telephone Inquiry Department

Another device for making the easy use of library resources is to establish a telephone inquiry department for the convenience of those who have not the time to visit the library. The inquiries received over the telephone over a wide range of subject and most of them may be answered immediately. If the preparation of answer takes up time, the questioner is rung up again. In this manner, the readers are also enable to inquire whether any desired book is available and sometimes the requests for re-issues are also complied.

Readers Advisory Service

The job of reader's advisor should be entrusted to those who have a wide knowledge of books and real liking for helping the people. The Readers Advisory Service should be carefully organized. The table of the Readers Advisor should be placed in a position where it is easily accessible. If possible, the table should be placed in the centre of a fairly spacious room where the public can move freely.

The Readers Advisor's table should be equipped with a telephone also. Near the Advisor's table facing the public there should be a notice inviting readers to make use the advisory service. At one side of the table should be a small book case for preserving small bibliographical reference aids and necessary files.

The newly enrolled members should be introduced to the Readers Advisor whose first job will be to find out the readers interest where relevant materials can be found in the stacks. He should also maintain the records of interest of new readers for future guide of book selection. Reader's suggestion and enquiries are of great importance for building up a satisfactory collection of reading materials. The suggestions should be sorted out once in a week and when the book required is purchased the readers may be informed. If the suggestion has been rejected the reason should be known to the reader. In order to make the library services effective, the Readers Advisory Service should be organized very efficiently.

Besides, now-a-days, all information regarding a particular library may be hosted on web-site as home page. This all will give wide publicity as well as the ways to use the particular library to its readers.